An excellent and thought-provoking approach to leadership, grounded in real military experience and brought to life through practical, relatable anecdotes. I would strongly recommend this book to leaders at any stage of their journey.

Lt Cdr Jacqueline 'Jack' McWilliams RN (retd)

All too often, books on 'leadership' are written from lofty heights, employing highly conceptual language and using examples beyond the remit of the vast majority of leaders. Chris Dodd's understanding of leadership has resulted in an uniquely relevant work that will be of immense, practical help to the 90 per cent of us who lead from less elevated levels than the 'usual' authors.

Cdre Nick Stanley RN (retd)

Navigating Leadership is an insightful and highly relevant guide for emerging leaders across both military and civilian professions. You'll explore and come to understand what truly effective leadership requires.

Sqn Ldr Sherry McBain ARRC PMRAFNS RAF (retd)

Reading books like this and preparing yourself can help you make the right decisions at the right time and achieve your goals.

Lt Cdr Anthony Ford RN (retd)

In over 30 years as a firefighter, I've seen how challenging the step into leadership can be. This book offers practical, honest guidance for those taking on that responsibility for the first time. Chris Dodd cuts through the theory and focuses on what truly matters: accountability, clarity and looking after your people.

George N Pendlington, Cleveland Fire Brigade DO (retd)

Drawing on real-world experience, Chris Dodd offers grounded leadership lessons that translate particularly well into healthcare and public service environments. A highly valuable book for firsttime leaders navigating responsibility, uncertainty and high expectations.

Helen Bromage, chief nursing information officer and registered nurse

This book provides a fascinating insight into the world of Royal Navy leadership. Drawing on personal experience over many years, Chris Dodd explores leadership and decision-making under pressure, unconscious bias, emotional discipline and building trust with colleagues in an easy-to-read and informative style. Much of the content is highly relevant across a wide range of professions. The appendices are especially useful and I'll be recommending it on our reading list for leadership in healthcare.

Prof Peter A Brennan OBE MD PhD FRCS, consultant surgeon and honorary professor of surgery

Navigating **Leadership**

Essential lessons from life at sea

Christopher Dodd

Navigating Leadership

ISBN 978-1-917490-30-6

eISBN 978-1-917490-31-3

Published in 2026 by Right Book Press

Printed in the UK in July 2026

Manufactured by
Sue Richardson Associates Ltd.
Studio 6,
9, Marsh Street
Bristol
BS1 4AA

info@therightbookcompany.com

A CIP record of this book is available from the British Library.

Disclaimer
No names, likenesses or ship identities in this book reflect real individuals or vessels. They've been changed or left vague to protect privacy, operational security and professional integrity. Any leadership models or frameworks referenced in this book are used for illustrative and educational purposes only and are described in the author's own words.

A note about truth

Every story, lesson and hard-earned scar in these pages did happen. The details may be adjusted for protection, but the experiences, challenges and insights are real, and they've shaped the leadership mindset I'm about to share with you.

This book is dedicated to the members of the British Armed Forces – the men, women and animals who serve day in, day out, often far from home, in support of this country and its people. It's also for their families, who stand beside them, carry the weight quietly and make that service possible.

Acknowledgements

I'd like to thank the many leaders I've had the privilege to serve with and under over the years. Some were outstanding and set the standard. Others were terrible and taught me just as much, often more, about how leadership should actually be done.

Every lesson in this book stems from those experiences.

— Chris

Contents

Appendices

Preface

If you're holding this book, you've already taken a big step. You want to lead, maybe for the first time, maybe better than before or maybe you've just been thrown into it and don't want to make an arse of yourself. Either way, you're in good company. Most leaders start out feeling underprepared, out of their depth or quietly hoping no one notices they're winging it.

I know that feeling well.

When I joined the Royal Navy (RN) in 2005, I was an unconfident, badly dyslexic lad from Teesside who, after leaving school, had spent five years in a back-street garage as an apprentice car mechanic, wondering what the hell I was going to do with my life. I wasn't academic, maths terrified me and I genuinely believed I'd never fit into an office job or anything that involved paperwork. Money was tight, confidence was low and life felt confusing. Everyone else seemed to know where they were going in life and I was stuck in the same place, trying to make sense of it all.

The job itself wasn't the issue. I loved the hands-on side of fixing cars and learning by doing. But the day-in, day-out monotony, the lack of direction, the feeling that I was just existing instead of actually living – that's what pushed me. I wanted the cliché: see the world, do something different and get paid to do it.

So, at 21, I joined the Navy, which is actually on the older side compared to a lot of people who go in at 16 or 18. I remember feeling as if I didn't have a plan: I was just going to go with the flow and see what happened, and I certainly didn't imagine I'd end up joining for as long as I did or being promoted as I was. I just knew I wanted a fresh start, a bit of discipline and a chance to prove something to myself.

If you're not familiar with the RN, it's worth knowing this: you're stepping into an organisation with more than 400 years of hard-earned experience in leadership under pressure. From places such as Portsmouth, Plymouth and Chatham, generations of sailors have learned how to operate, survive and lead when mistakes cost lives, ships or missions. Figures like Nelson didn't shape the Navy through slogans, but through decisions made in uncertainty, responsibility taken at personal cost and standards held when it would've been easier to bend them. You don't need to know the history to understand this book, but it helps explain why the Navy takes leadership so seriously. A lot of what you'll read here has been tested, broken, rebuilt and passed down over centuries – not in classrooms, but at sea, under pressure.

Like most people joining the military, I had this *Full Metal Jacket* idea of basic training in my head. A gunnery sergeant shouting obscenities at me. Strict discipline. Getting beasted around the parade ground. I thought that was the whole point, that leadership in the Navy was going to be about volume and attitude. Spoiler: it wasn't.

I didn't sail straight into my branch of choice, either. I wanted to be a marine engineer (ME), but I failed the joining test. I sat in the careers office, opened the exam paper and panic took over the second I saw that the first question was a maths one. The whole thing went downhill from there. Luckily, the careers office called me back and said I could join as a warfare rating (WR, essentially a junior enlisted sailor). It wasn't what I'd hoped for, but it got me in the door, and that was all I needed.

So, that was me off to HMS *Raleigh* to start basic training, and it flew by. Before long, I was at HMS *Collingwood*, the Maritime Warfare School, for phase two training: ops room work, seamanship skills and upper-deck routines. I gave it everything, but deep down, it didn't feel like the right fit. My first ship, a Type 42 destroyer, was about to deploy for six months to the Falklands. Most of my time on board as a young warfare rating (WR) was spent greasing, sweeping up after smokers on the quarterdeck and doing jobs that didn't scratch the itch I had for engineering.

It wasn't that I didn't like the ship; it was a good ship with a good crew. But I knew I wasn't in the right world. Every time I saw the stokers working away, going in and out of the engine rooms and machinery spaces in their overalls and carrying tools, I knew they were doing the kind of work I understood. And I couldn't shake the feeling that I was in the wrong branch. I'd joined the Navy to get stuck into fixing machinery, proper hands-on engineering, and that's where I wanted to be.

And that's when my luck changed. Word had got around that the lad in the warfare branch had been a car mechanic before joining. The marine engineering officer called me in, looked at my NVQs, and the next day I was sent down to the stokers' mess with new branch badges, a task book to crack on with and the proud new title of MEM2 Dodd. For the first time since joining, something clicked. Engines. Machinery. Work I could enjoy. It made sense to me. It was where I belonged. Without realising it, this was where I took my first steps towards leadership.

After the Falklands deployment, I had completed most of my task book on board, but what I didn't realise was that I still had to go back through the formal engineering training at HMS *Sultan* to get the proper qualification. So, I left my first ship and headed to Gosport to join a new course of phase-two recruits straight from *Raleigh*. Unlike the others on the course, I had already been to sea, so at least I knew what the kit and equipment we were learning about actually looked like in real life. Once I passed the training phase, I was drafted to another Type 42 destroyer, my first proper ship as a marine engineering mechanic (MEM).

This ship was a different world. The stokers' mess was full of morale, humour and camaraderie. I loved it. And quite quickly, I was given more responsibility than I expected. The ship was short of leading hands in the engineering department, and because I had shown I could crack on and get the job done, I was made local acting leading hand (LH). That meant doing the job without having done the course yet, but I didn't care – I'd been there, done that as an MEM2. I was chuffed. It was my first proper leadership role, running the mess and looking after the junior rate (JR) stokers day to day.

This was where I took my first real steps into leadership.

I eventually got where I wanted to be. The Navy gave me a

fresh start, but not in the way I expected. I learned at the start that leadership wasn't about shouting orders, marching people around or the kind of nonsense you see in films. It was about people: understanding them, supporting them, getting the best out of them when it mattered. And that meant earning trust long before you ever relied on rank.

One of the first lessons came when I became 'killick of the mess'. We had captain's rounds coming up and the mess deck needed to be spotless. I got the lads stuck in cleaning the way I thought would get them working at sea: music on, beer fridge open, banter flowing, everyone grafting away cleaning the mess square and their own bunk spaces. The mess was looking decent. When one lad told me his bunk was clean and squared away, being new in the role I took him at his word.

The next day, the captain arrived and I proudly reported the mess ready for his inspection. And of course, the first bunk he checked was that lad's. He lifted the mattress and found the full horror show underneath. Old socks, sweet wrappers, magazines, the lot. My jaw hit the deck.

To his credit, the captain didn't tear into me. He could see I was new to the job and embarrassed. He simply said, 'You can deal with him', and moved on.

And deal with him I did. The lad was kit-mustered. After rounds, I thanked the rest of the mess for their hard work because the space was spotless apart from that one bunk. No grudges, no drama. He cocked up, he got corrected and we moved on. But the lesson stuck: never report something as ready unless you've seen it with your own eyes.

It sounds like a small moment, but it shaped how I led from then on. Real leadership isn't glamorous or dramatic. It is responsibility. If your name is on it, you own it. And if you want standards, you have to check standards. It was the first time I realised that leadership lives in the small moments, not the big speeches.

Throughout my nearly 19 years in the RN, through deployments, crises, engineering faults, long nights and tougher days, I learned that leadership isn't fixed. You build it through experience, reflection, mistakes and momentum. Sometimes you learn from brilliant leaders. More often, you learn from the bad ones, the ones who lead with rank instead of respect. Funnily enough, those people taught me more about the kind of leader I didn't want to be than any textbook ever could.

That is one of the main reasons I wrote this book. Because the reality is that leadership isn't taught through PowerPoint slides or laminated values posters. It is taught in real moments, real mistakes and under real pressure. And I wish someone had told me half of this when I started. I wrote this for the new leaders who feel like I did back then, unsure, nervous, desperate to get it right but terrified of getting it wrong.

What matters whether you're leading sailors, apprentices, care workers, software teams or the night shift in a warehouse:

Leadership is human. Not military. Not corporate. Human.

The tools and mindset in this book aren't based on theory. They are based on nearly two decades of real-world leadership under pressure – what worked, what didn't and what I wish someone had told me when I first stepped into the role.

This book isn't a novel. You don't need to read it front to back. Pick a chapter when you need it. Use the tools, the stories, the mindset. Take what works, bin what doesn't and adapt it for your world.

And don't worry about the Navy slang and terminology. There's a glossary at the back if you get lost. I am not going to water down the Jack speak. It is part of who I am and how I lead.

If you're stepping into leadership for the first time, especially if you feel nervous, underprepared or like you're going to be found out, remember this. Every leader starts there. Confidence comes with time, practice and understanding, not perfection.

Leadership isn't about being perfect. It's about showing up, learning and leading well when it counts.

You bring the drive. I'll bring the tools. Let's crack on.

Chapter 1

The unique nature of Royal Navy leadership

The RN is steeped in history and tradition, yet it remains a living system built on evolving leadership. The foundation of the RN as an institution is generally traced to the mid-16th century under Henry VIII, when the 'Navy Royal' was formally established and England's sea power began to take shape. Over the following centuries, this force evolved from its early defensive duties into a dominant global naval power, driven by advances in ship design, navigation and strategy.

However, with growth came complexity. From sails to steam engines, radar and nuclear propulsion, every innovation raised the bar for those in charge. Leadership in the Navy has never been just about rank. It's about decision making under pressure, building trust in unpredictable conditions and adapting fast when the plan changes.

Junior leaders often carry significant responsibility. Whether it's guiding a team through a high-pressure operation or managing a vital section of the ship, their decisions can make or break both mission success and morale. This was just as true during the Second World War, when limited communication meant junior officers often had to make critical decisions without waiting for orders from above – leading through chaos, uncertainty and immense pressure. The same level of autonomy and accountability still exists today.

At senior levels, leadership becomes more strategic. It's about managing long-range objectives, navigating uncertainty and inspiring people through vision rather than just authority. Think of Admiral Lord Nelson at the Battle of Trafalgar: not just a tactician, but a motivator who led from the front and kept his team united under fire.

What the Navy teaches and what I learnt first hand is that leadership isn't bound by age or position. It's measured by trust, clarity and your ability to act under pressure. Whether you're managing ten people or ten thousand, the fundamentals don't change: communicate clearly, earn trust and make decisions that bring people with you.

In 2022, I was serving on board a Hunt-class mine hunter, mid-transit in the Arabian Gulf, skirting the edge of Iranian territorial waters. The sun had just gone down. It was calm, routine, one of those rare evenings where you think you might actually get a quiet watch. I'd literally just sat down after being told everything was fine in my handover.

Then the ship went black.

Both running generators had tripped offline due to overheating. The back-up failed to start. Suddenly, we had no power. No navigation. No comms. No lights. Just a minehunter drifting in a sensitive area with no way to steer and no way to call for help.

One thing the Navy teaches you fast is that when the lights go out, people want answers immediately. Within seconds, the bridge was on the internal comms. The officer of the watch needed to brief the captain. Were we drifting towards Iranian waters? Was this a fault or something bigger? What was happening down in the machinery spaces?

Here's the thing, though. When the power failed, it was as much of a surprise to me as it was to them. The difference was that my department and I were the ones who had to fix it. As the engine room petty officer (PO) I was responsible for the propulsion plant, the main engines and the machinery that kept the ship alive. My lads were already heading for the generator room, and I knew piling pressure on them would be dangerous. They needed space to assess, move safely and get me the facts. So I kept it simple and said the only thing I could say with confidence.

'Bridge, we've lost both generators. I'll update ASAP.'

Absorbing the pressure so they didn't have to.

They didn't need micromanaging. They needed me to hold the line above so they could fix the problem below. They checked in straight away, told me what they could and cracked on.

That's what leadership looks like in real time. Not pretending you have all the answers but staying composed, owning the situation and trusting the people you've trained. You won't always get it perfect, but hesitating or guessing under pressure can be far worse than taking calm, informed action.

The chapters that follow unpack those lessons and link them to civilian life, because whether you're stepping into your first team lead role or running an organisation, the same core skills apply.

1.1: Teamwork and collaboration

In the RN, teamwork is a way of life. Every operation, from routine duties to international deployments, depends on it. Whether you're navigating hostile waters or delivering aid after a disaster, success comes down to how well people work together. Regardless of rank or rate, when it hits the fan, we really are all in the same boat.

The strongest teams I served with had common traits: open communication, mutual trust and role clarity. Everyone knew their part and knew they'd be supported when it counted. Real leadership is not about controlling every detail; it's about enabling people to do their best work.

The RN trains constantly for the unexpected: fires, floods, mechanical failures. However, sometimes, it's not a drill. It's the real thing.

As a young leading hand, I was dealing with a genuine emergency: a high-pressure saltwater pipe where the fire main had burst, flooding one of the compartments. I was on the upper deck, managing the response and issuing instructions across the team.

Before I could give the order, an AB in the compartment below made a snap decision and isolated the leaking section of pipe. Now, isolating a fire main isn't a call you make lightly. That line could've been in use elsewhere; cutting it off without clearance could have left another firefighting team without water. However, he had assessed the situation and knew there was no fire forward (or did he?). He also knew that if we didn't stop the leak immediately, the compartment would flood and we'd lose not just the space, but vital equipment.

When I asked him why he didn't wait for my order, he simply replied: 'Mate, if we'd waited, we'd have lost the compartment and everything in it.'

And he was right. But he was also wrong.

He broke procedure, but for the right reasons. He'd made a call under pressure, and it was the right one (in this situation). Still, I knew that decision could land him in hot water with others in the chain of command. So I defended him, explained the context and stood by his judgement.

We weren't in a war zone. No one was in immediate danger. What he showed was initiative, awareness and confidence under pressure. That's what we should encourage. That moment reminded me that leadership is not about enforcing rules. It's about knowing when the situation demands flexibility.

From that day on, I paid more attention to insight, not just authority. Time and again, I saw that stepping back and letting someone with the right knowledge take the lead made the team stronger. That's not weakness – that's leadership.

Good teams don't just respond to orders. They adapt, anticipate and solve problems together. But only if the environment allows it. Leaders need to read the room, notice when someone's off, when tension's rising, when feedback is missing. These signals are more revealing than any formal review.

Real teamwork creates the kind of space where people can perform, recover and thrive. That starts with you, the leader.

1.2: Adaptability and resilience

In life, change is a given and pressure can be constant. In the RN, that's your baseline. Whether it was a mission being redirected overnight, kit breaking mid-op or having to function on minimal sleep, something always shifts just when you think you've got a grip on things.

In those moments, adaptability isn't helpful – it's essential.

When something breaks, you fix it. When plans change, you regroup. You don't wait for perfect conditions. You act with what you have. That mindset transfers straight into civilian leadership. Whether it's supply chain issues, market shifts or people suddenly leaving, the challenge is the same: uncertainty. Leaders who panic lose the room. The ones who stay calm, rally their team and shift gears with confidence become the anchor in the storm.

Resilience goes hand in hand with adaptability. It means pushing through, learning from setbacks and showing your team that pressure sharpens you rather than breaks you. Nobody enjoys discomfort, but great leaders lean into it and come out stronger.

The night the generators failed taught me something that stayed with me. People up the chain want answers fast, but they don't always appreciate how hard it is for the people below to get those answers safely. As a young stoker, I'd felt that pressure. As a PO, I absorbed it so my JRs didn't have to. That's the job. Trust your team, give them space to work and they'll get you the information you need, as long as you've led them well.

Even now, in civilian work, those same principles guide me: stay flexible, stay grounded and keep improving.

1.3: Morale

Morale is the heartbeat of any team. In the RN, it's critical. High morale keeps teams motivated, sharp and cohesive. Low morale? That's when things start to unravel, communication breaks down, performance drops and trust erodes.

I've seen what happens when morale is neglected. I was deployed on a NATO exercise in the Mediterranean – on paper, a high-profile, prestigious tasking. In practice, it was three months of being worked to the bone. The ship had already spent months training hard around UK waters before deployment, and by the time we arrived in theatre, the crew was already worn down.

From the outset, it was all stick, no carrot. Because we were part of a visible NATO task group, our ship was volunteered for every available task, whether at sea or alongside. Downtime was practically non-existent. The focus was entirely on appearances:

drills, inspections, functions, more functions, and let's not forget the seventh cocktail party in a row.

At first, people tried to keep the humour alive. Over time, though, the jokes dried up and the laughter faded. You could feel the disengagement creeping in. Even the best among us began clock-watching, like civilians in an office waiting for home time, except home was still three months away.

Crew stopped volunteering. But that didn't mean they were left alone. The answer was simple: *if you didn't volunteer, you would be voluntold.*

Mistakes began to happen, not from lack of skill, but from sheer fatigue and disconnection. Morale didn't collapse in a dramatic explosion. It decayed in silence, a slow leak, and that's what makes it so dangerous. You don't always see it coming until it's already sunk in.

It wasn't just the commanding officer (CO). The wardroom felt young and inexperienced. Many officers seemed reluctant to speak up, likely focused on doing what was needed to progress their career. That perception wasn't just mine; it was echoed across the mess decks. Even senior rates (SRs), normally a backbone of morale, seemed disengaged. And when junior leaders tried to lift the crew, they were held back. It felt as if those above were struggling and didn't want those below to be doing any better.

However, I've also seen what happens when morale is nurtured.

A good team doesn't need motivational posters in their place of work; they need clarity, consistency and a reason to care. Leaders who listen, who communicate clearly, who give people room to take ownership and then recognise their effort – those are the ones who build crews that thrive.

Thriving teams back each other. They still want to eat together, laugh together, work together, even under pressure. That sense of unity is what carries you through tough deployments, and it doesn't happen by accident. It's built by leaders who understand that morale isn't soft; it's operationally critical.

You set the emotional tone of your team. If you carry stress, anger or detachment, it spreads like smoke through ventilation. If you bring calm, energy and presence, your team will reflect that back. Your job as a leader is to create the conditions where people care: about the job, about each other and about doing their best.

1.4: Practices and theories

Leadership isn't wizardry; it's a skill you can graft at like anything else. Yes, some people have natural presence or confidence, but long-term, effective leadership is built on principles, not personality. The Navy gave me plenty of chances to test those principles. While the environment could be extreme, the models we used translate well to civilian life.

Three notable ones are:

Style	**Summary/characteristics**
Situational leadership	No one size fits all
Charismatic leadership	Powerful but risky
Democratic leadership	Shared power builds commitment

Forget the theory: these models actually work if you bend them to your team. The key is to take the theory, apply it to your context and refine it as you go.

1.5: Balancing discipline and openness

One of the hardest things to master in leadership is finding the balance between structure and flexibility. In the Navy, the default is discipline: chain of command, clear rules, no room for ambiguity, and for good reasons. But even in a high-stakes environment, I found that too much control creates silence. People stop speaking up. They follow instructions but stop thinking. That's when problems go unnoticed or, worse, get ignored.

Real leadership happens when you blend accountability with approachability. When your team knows where the line is but also know they can speak their mind. That kind of openness builds trust and often surfaces your best ideas.

This one's a bit off topic, but ask any proud engineer, and they'll tell you: we get attached to our machines. I'm no different. When I was a PO responsible for the propulsion system on board a certain MCMV, those two powerful V16 diesel engines were my babies. One day, I hit an ECU (engine control unit) fault. The fix? A complete software wipe and fresh upload to the control unit. Should've been straightforward. Except it wasn't, for me.

I found the whole process confusing and frustrating. Computers are not my thing. I knew the engine inside and out, but the software side left me feeling out of my depth. That's when a young AB, one of the weapons lads, stepped up. He'd never worked on engines, but he understood software, and that's what I needed.

Even though I knew I needed the help, I found it hard to let go. This was *my* engine. *My* responsibility. I should've been the one fixing it. Instead, I was stuck and the JR was unfazed, calm and quietly getting on with the job. But as he started the upload process, I caught myself doing something I didn't like. I was hovering, overexplaining, questioning steps, unintentionally micromanaging him and slowing everything down.

It wasn't that I didn't trust him. It was that I couldn't quite get past my own ego. I needed to be reassured *he* wasn't going to mess up *my* engine. The irony, of course, was that I couldn't do it myself. Eventually, I stepped back, gave him space and of course he sorted it perfectly. Upload complete. Engine back online. No fuss, no drama.

That experience taught me something:

- ⚓ Leadership means *knowing when you're the right person for the job and when you're not.*
- ⚓ It means checking your ego, letting people show what they can do and creating space for others to succeed.

And sometimes, it means watching a junior lad do in five minutes what you've been struggling with for an hour.

The civilian world demands this even more. Hierarchies are flatter. People expect transparency. If you rely solely on control, you'll lose your best people. But if you lead with only openness and no structure, you lose alignment. Balance is the skill.

1.6: Military vs civilian leadership

Military leadership is built on order, clarity and accountability. Civilian leadership often runs on collaboration, creativity and flexibility. Both have strengths and both have blind spots.

In the Navy, you know exactly who's in charge, what's expected and what happens when the standard isn't met. That structure drives efficiency and safety, especially in high-risk environments. Civilian settings are different. Decisions often involve consensus. Roles aren't always fixed. People want to feel heard. It can feel messier, but it also allows for more agility and innovation.

For me, the transition into a civilian work environment wasn't about abandoning Navy lessons; it was about translating them. The clarity I learned around communication, decision making and accountability still applies. However, the way you deliver those things shifts; you don't just give orders. You invite buy-in. In short: structure still matters, but so does empathy. Get both right and you've got a leadership style that works in any environment.

Chapter 2

Leading with purpose

In the Royal Navy, everything is tied to something bigger: service, defence, duty and each other. Leading with purpose is about helping people understand why their work matters and guiding them with meaning, direction and shared values.

Purpose gives your leadership weight. It motivates people to act when things get tough and connects the day-to-day grind to something bigger than the job list. When people see where they fit in the bigger picture, they perform better. Not because they have to, but because they want to.

2.1: Traditional vs purpose-driven leadership

Traditional leadership tends to focus on results, rank and compliance. It works, especially in structured environments, but it can miss the human element. You might hit performance targets, but morale and engagement will suffer if people don't understand the why behind what they're doing.

Purpose-driven leadership, on the other hand, is different. It balances goals with meaning. It's about aligning your team's work with values, mission and a sense of contribution. A good captain doesn't just issue orders. They explain why those orders matter to the mission, to the team and to something bigger than any one person.

And it's the same in civilian life. People will give more, push further and grow faster when they believe what they do matters. That's purpose. It's what turns a job into something people care about.

2.2: Adapting your leadership style

Some leaders rely on one leadership style no matter the context. The best ones don't. They adapt based on the team, the moment and the mission.

Think about it: in a crisis, you might need to lead decisively and take charge. But in a planning session, listening and drawing ideas from the team gets better results. Leadership is situational, and your ability to flex your style is one of your most important tools.

You don't need to master every style overnight. But you do need to understand three things:

- which styles come naturally to you
- which ones challenge you
- when each style is most effective.

What works in a calm planning meeting might fall flat during a crisis. Sometimes, you need a firm, autocratic hand. Other times, the smartest move is stepping back and letting your team think and breathe.

What follows are eight leadership styles, each with its own strengths and limitations. I've included military and civilian examples for each to show how they play out in different environments. You'll probably recognise yourself in more than one of these. That's normal and good. The goal here isn't to label yourself, but to become more aware of how you lead, where you're strongest and where you can adapt.

The leadership styles below are widely recognised across military leadership training, organisational psychology and management practice. They draw on established work by thinkers such as Kurt Lewin, Max Weber, James MacGregor Burns and Robert Greenleaf, as well as modern leadership development approaches. I am not presenting this as theory for theory's sake, just as practical ways of thinking about leadership that you will see used every day, whether people realise it or not.

Let's break them down.

	What it is	When to use	Example	Strengths	Weaknesses
Autocratic	Decisions made by the leader; no team input.	Emergencies, tight control environments.	Ship's CO during combat or a CEO in a crisis.	Fast decisions, clear authority.	Can stifle creativity and morale if overused.
Bureaucratic	Rule-based, process-focused, by the book.	High-risk or regulated environments.	XO during inspections or a compliance officer.	Ensures consistency, discipline and safety.	Can be rigid, slow to adapt, discourages initiative.
Charismatic	Motivating through energy, vision and personal connection.	Inspiring change, building morale.	Junior officer rallying crew, start-up founder.	Boosts engagement and loyalty.	Over-reliance on personality, potential ego risks.
Democratic	Involving the team in decisions.	Collaborative planning, building ownership.	Leading hand gathering input or team feedback sessions.	Builds trust, encourages innovation.	Slower decisions, can frustrate fast movers.
Laissez-Faire	Hands-off leadership, high autonomy for the team.	With skilled, self-driven teams.	Warrant officer trusting SRs or a creative tech team.	Encourages ownership and innovation.	Risk of drift, lack of accountability without structure.
Servant	Putting the team's needs first, leading through service.	People development, welfare, coaching.	CPO mentoring sailors or an HR leader supporting wellbeing.	Builds trust, empathy, long-term loyalty.	Can lead to burnout or blurred authority lines.
Transactional	Performance-based, reward and punishment focused.	Task execution, KPIs, short-term goals.	Officer managing conduct or sales-focused manager.	Clear expectations, results focused.	Doesn't build deep engagement or creativity.
Transformational	Inspiring big-picture change and personal growth.	Vision-setting, cultural change, innovation.	Visionary skipper or a CEO leading transformation.	Drives growth, meaning and long term success.	Can lack practical grounding or short term discipline.

2.3: What kind of leader are you?

Let me give you a few examples from my own time in uniform and beyond. These aren't theory. They're moments that showed me how different leadership styles apply depending on the situation, the people, the pressure and the moment.

Charismatic and motivating: I once watched a senior officer deliver news nobody wanted to hear. Our deployment had already been six months long and, two weeks before we were due home, it was extended by another two.

Instead of sending a formal message or hiding behind rank, he came down to the mess deck, sat with us and spoke like a human being. He didn't sugar-coat it, but he didn't dodge it either. He used humour, empathy and straight talk.

We weren't happy about the extension. But we respected him for how he handled it. And afterwards, the mess felt more united. That's charisma used properly.

Servant leadership in action: Some of my proudest moments in leadership didn't come from technical wins. They came from stopping good people from slipping through the cracks.

One sailor I worked with was ready to leave the Navy – not because she didn't enjoy the job; she loved it. She was reliable and hard working. The problem was promotion. She was missing some academic qualifications and had convinced herself she couldn't pass the exams, so why bother? Over time, that frustration turned into 'maybe I should just get out'.

Rather than telling her to crack on or pushing her out, I stepped back and listened. We broke it down properly – the qualifications she was missing, the exams she needed, how she could tackle the studying alongside the job. We put a plan together that felt manageable.

Six months later, she passed her leading hand's board. A year after that, she wore her new rate with pride.

That wasn't my win. It was hers. But it showed me something important. Servant leadership doesn't just develop people. It keeps good people in the organisation. Sometimes all it takes is helping someone navigate the bit they struggle with.

Transformational in civilian life: Leaving the Navy meant adjusting how I lead – not abandoning what I'd learned, but applying it differently. The pace is faster in some ways, messier in others. People are dealing with change, uncertainty and a lot of noise.

You do not need all the answers to lead well. Sometimes the job is to help people slow things down, see the bigger picture and make sense of what is in front of them, giving teams enough clarity and confidence to move forward even when the situation is not clear.

At its core, it's the same leadership. Trust your people. Be clear about direction. Give them purpose when things feel uncertain. The environment's changed, but the principles haven't.

So, everyone has a dominant leadership style, one that feels natural and comfortable. But the best leaders don't stay stuck in default mode. They recognise their go-to style, then stretch their range. They lead with intention, not habit. And they adapt their approach to meet the moment, no matter the setting.

You'll find a leadership style self-assessment in Appendix A. The point is to build self-awareness. When you understand your natural tendencies, you can make smarter, more conscious choices about how you lead, especially when pressure hits or circumstances shift.

You do not lead well by clinging to a fixed plan or a favourite method. You lead well by turning up with purpose and choosing the right tone, the right tools and the right mindset, again and again. Whether you're barking orders on a ship's upper deck or guiding a project team in a boardroom, your purpose is your compass. Without it, leadership becomes hollow. With it, leadership becomes grounded and effective. Keep that in mind. Let it shape not just what you do, but how you lead, every day.

Keep that in mind. Let it shape not just what you do, but *how* you lead, every day.

Chapter 3

Building trust and loyalty

Trust and loyalty aren't instilled in training or on the parade square. They're built in the spaces in between, often when no one's watching and no one's giving orders. On one occasion we were alongside Gibraltar after a long stint at sea. Everyone was ready for a blowout. Spirits were high. Beers were flowing. The whole crew needed a reset.

But one of the lads took it too far.

You know the type – quiet on board, never a problem. But give him a few pints and suddenly he's a hand grenade with the pin out. Two hours in, he was slurring, stumbling and on the verge of being picked up by the local police. In short, he was being an arse. He wasn't in any fit state to get back to the ship and couldn't be trusted to do so alone.

I'll be honest: my first reaction wasn't some saintly leadership response. At first I laughed and thought, 'For f***'s sake, how's he got this drunk this fast?' Then the amusement wore off and the concern kicked in. And underneath that was the selfish thought a lot of people have but don't admit: 'Thank God it's not me taking him back – I want to enjoy my night.' Those honest, human reactions are real, but they can't be where you stop as a leader.

In theory, this is where a good leader steps up and takes him back. And let's be honest, no one joins the Navy dreaming of ending their night babysitting a pissed-up shipmate. It's easy to say, 'He's made his bed, let him lie in it.'

But that's not what happened.

One of his messmates stepped in – no fuss, no orders, no ego. He quietly got him up, got him in a taxi and made sure he got back on board without incident – no drama, no lectures, no grassing. Just handled it. It wasn't about covering anything up. It was about knowing when someone's had a wobble and stepping in to protect the person and the team.

If he'd been left to his own devices, the fallout could've been worse: trouble with the locals, disciplinary action, damage to the ship's reputation. That one small act probably saved him from a world of pain. And more than that, it shows what loyalty really looks like.

Someone explained it to me like this years ago, and it stuck: 'he might be a d***, but he's our d***'. That doesn't excuse bad behaviour, but it does mean we look after our own and deal with it the right way. That's the kind of quiet loyalty that builds trust you can rely on when it really counts.

You don't earn trust with a job title. You earn it by having your team's back when they need it most, on watch, in a crisis or flat on their face outside a bar in Gib. And when your people know you'd do the same for them? That's when leadership truly sticks.

3.1: Why trust matters

Trust is the cornerstone of effective leadership, whether you're commanding a warship, running a school or managing a project team. In high-pressure, high-responsibility environments, trust isn't optional – it's survival.

At sea, we trust our team to make split-second decisions, often without orders. They trust us to lead them with fairness, clarity and competence. And that mutual trust? It's what keeps people safe, systems running and missions on track.

That principle holds just as true on land. Whether you're leading engineers, analysts or frontline responders, your people need to trust you. They need to trust *each other.* That's how you build cohesion, solve problems under pressure and navigate uncertainty.

And here's the key; trust doesn't come from a uniform, a title or a nameplate on the door. It's built through action, day by day, under stress and often when it's least convenient.

3.2: Building trust in high-stakes environments

In the Navy, trust is built in moments both big and small. It starts with transparency, clear communication and no hidden agendas. It's reinforced through reliability, doing what you said you'd do, every time. And it's strengthened through fairness, treating your people with consistency, respect and integrity.

When leaders say one thing and do another, trust crumbles. When they blame others or protect their ego at the team's expense, people shut down. But when they lead with honesty, own their decisions and support their team, even when things go wrong, trust grows.

In civilian teams, the stakes may not be life or death, but the principle holds. Teams that trust each other solve problems faster, take initiative and stay motivated when challenges arise. Leaders who are trusted don't need to chase updates constantly; their teams bring them the truth without fear.

3.3: Leading with emotional intelligence

You can't build trust without emotional intelligence. As a leader, you're constantly being observed, not just for *what* you say but *how* you say it and how you carry yourself when the pressure mounts, the rules change or the circumstances feel unfair.

Emotional intelligence (EQ) is your ability to recognise and manage your own emotions while staying attuned to those of others. It includes:

- **self-awareness** – recognising your own emotional triggers and behavioural patterns
- **self-regulation** – keeping your composure when it matters most
- **empathy** – understanding and responding to how others feel, even when they don't voice it.

These aren't 'soft skills' – they're core leadership traits.

Psychologist Daniel Goleman, who helped popularise the modern idea of emotional intelligence in leadership, breaks EQ into areas such as self-awareness, self-control, motivation, empathy and social skill. You don't need to start studying his academic research papers, but it's worth knowing that there's solid research behind it. Studies across business and public service (eg CIPD 2023) show that leaders who score higher on EQ tend to build more trust, keep people for longer and get stronger performance over time.

Some people seem naturally wired to pick up on emotional shifts. They walk into a workplace and instantly feel that something's off. To others it doesn't come so easily. Either way, it's a skill, not a magic gift. You develop it the same way you develop anything else in leadership: by paying attention, reflecting when you get it wrong and deliberately trying to notice more than just the task in front of you.

Most of us default to quickly labelling people: they're moody, they're being awkward, they've got a bad attitude today. Leaders with emotional intelligence ask a different question: 'What might be going on underneath this?' Very often it isn't attitude at all – it's tiredness, pressure, worry or someone quietly carrying something heavy that you can't see.

At the other end of the scale, you do get people with almost no EQ who still climb the ladder, the cold, ultra-rational types who never seem flustered. On paper they can look like great leaders: decisive, focused, ruthless under pressure. But without emotional intelligence they usually get short-term compliance, not long-term loyalty. People follow them because they have to, not because they want to.

On the other hand, leaders who deliberately build their EQ learn to read the room and adjust. They notice when humour dries up, when someone goes quiet who's usually chatty or when a team that used to crack on suddenly starts dragging its heels. That early warning lets you step in, ask a simple 'You all right?' and deal with the real issue before it turns into a crisis.

In 2021, during the height of the Covid-19 pandemic, many people across the UK were told to stay home. But not everyone had that option. As part of the regeneration of a certain warship, my engineering team and I were required to work on board. The ship needed to return to operational readiness and time was against us.

We were operating under new health and safety protocols, reduced manning and compressed timelines. Tensions were high. Morale was fragile. The team standing in front of me at morning stand-up weren't just tired, they were frustrated. Some couldn't understand why they were being asked to come in while other departments, in their eyes, were 'allowed' to work from home. To them, the situation felt unfair and inconsistent.

I delivered the brief as I normally would, outlining the tasks, timelines and broader mission. But it landed flat. Dismissive remarks and a lack of eye contact said more than words. The usual RN mindset of 'just get it done' wasn't cutting through. The crew weren't just confused; they were emotionally checked out.

Inside, I was feeling a lot of what they were: frustration and fatigue. And to be honest I was thinking, 'I don't really want to be here either.' But whether I liked it or not, I had to be seen to be getting on with it. On top of that, the pressure was real. We were undermanned, the deadlines were tight and the rules seemed to change almost daily. Everyone had their own spin on the latest guidance, trying to force old routines into a new reality instead of admitting, 'Maybe this can't be done the usual way.'

My first instinct? Frustration. It would've been easy to snap into directive mode: 'Stop complaining and crack on.' But that wouldn't have helped anyone. Instead, I paused. I reflected. I recognised that pressing ahead without empathy wasn't leadership; it was noise.

This didn't mean lowering expectations. It didn't mean being soft. It meant acknowledging the team's concerns while helping them to refocus on the bigger picture: why the task mattered, why *they* mattered and how their efforts would contribute to operational readiness and unit pride.

Covid also highlighted something I'd seen for years but never really named. There can be a real reluctance in the chain of command to be the bearer of bad news. Very few people want to go up the line and say, 'Sir, I don't think we can achieve this in the time or with the resources we've got.' They worry it makes them look weak or incompetent. So instead, the message becomes 'We'll just crack on' and the hidden cost is a team that quietly breaks under the strain. That was a big leadership lesson for me during my time in the Navy. Sometimes the bravest thing you can do is speak the unpopular truth early, before your people pay for it.

To guide my approach, I used **Driscoll's model of reflection** (2007). This helped me break down what happened, how I responded, and how I could adjust my leadership in real time. I also drew from **Lewin's change management model** (1947) focusing on the first stage: unfreeze. The team needed time to let go of how things *used* to work before they could adapt to the new normal.

People don't just follow your orders; they follow your *example*. If you can remain calm, clear headed and empathetic under stress, your team is far more likely to do the same.

Emotional intelligence does not mean acting all warm and fuzzy. It means staying sharp, composed and adaptable when it counts. You don't need to carry everyone's emotions, but you do need to manage your own. That steady presence builds the trust you'll need to lead through anything.

3.4: Emotional discipline in leadership

Leadership doesn't mean being emotionless – it means being emotionally disciplined. You're allowed to feel frustration, disappointment or stress. You're human, not a machine. What matters is *how* you express those emotions, whether you channel them constructively or let them leak out in ways that undermine your authority or damage your team.

The most effective leaders stay composed under pressure, even when they're internally raging, doubting or worn out. They take a breath, pause before reacting and choose their response carefully. That doesn't mean bottling everything up or pretending all is well; it means being *intentional* about when and how you respond.

Your team takes cues from you. If you snap, lash out or withdraw into silence, that emotional energy spreads fast. But if you model calm, controlled behaviour, especially in high-stress environments, they'll often match your tone.

That said, *controlling* your emotions doesn't mean *suppressing* them. Everyone needs a pressure release valve. Sometimes, walking away and letting off steam in private, yes, even if that means silently screaming into a pillow or towel, is exactly what you need to reset. Get it out, regain control, then return with clarity.

Self-discipline doesn't just build trust; it builds credibility. When your team sees that you can lead with calm clarity, even when things get tough, they'll have far more confidence in your leadership.

3.5: Handling team emotions

The best leaders don't just manage tasks; they manage people. And people come with emotions. There's been a growing mindset in recent years that other people's feelings, reactions or opinions aren't your concern. But if you want to succeed as a leader, they are.

You can see it in how expectations have shifted. When I first joined, you were told to do something and you did it. End of. Now, more and more, people expect an explanation, not just an order. The Navy has even formalised this with the idea of a 'reasonable challenge' culture, where anyone, regardless of rank, can question an order or raise a concern if they don't understand the rationale or think something might be unsafe. Used well, it stops mistakes and encourages people to think, not just obey. Used badly, it can slow things down or be seen as answering back. As a leader, your job is to strike a balance: encourage sensible challenge without losing momentum.

You can have the best plan in the world, but if your team's morale is crumbling, or if someone's carrying stress, doubt or distraction, things will unravel fast. Great leaders don't just track output; they pay attention to the atmosphere in the room, not just the actions on the task list.

I've lost count of the number of times I've walked into a brief or meeting and felt something was off long before anyone said it out loud. The plan itself was fine, but the body language was flat, the usual humour was gone or people were suddenly very quiet. In those moments, you've got a choice: ignore it and plough on, or pause and ask, 'What's actually going on here?' The times I stopped, acknowledged it and let people air what was bothering them, the plan usually stayed the same, but their willingness to get behind it changed completely.

This means noticing when someone's off their game. It means reading tone, picking up on body language and knowing when to ask 'Are you all right?' and mean it. Sometimes, your job is to listen. Other times, it's to steady the ship with clear direction. The real skill lies in knowing which to do and when.

When you work closely with a team for any length of time, you start to pick up on patterns. You know when they're happy, distracted, stressed or, let's be honest, when they just can't be arsed. That awareness is part of leadership.

Some emotions are easy to spot: frustration, anxiety, resistance. Others are more subtle: withdrawal, forced agreement or silence where there should be questions. You need to notice both. That doesn't mean you're the team therapist. It means staying present, approachable and tuned into what's going on beneath the surface. Strong leaders support their teams without carrying the emotional weight for them. They acknowledge concerns without letting those concerns derail momentum. They help their people feel seen, heard and valued, which in turn builds trust, loyalty and cohesion.

And this doesn't just apply in the military. In civilian teams, the leaders who can read the room and respond with a mix of honesty and empathy are the ones people choose to follow, even when they could just do the bare minimum and go home.

3.6: Camaraderie

On a warship, there's a bond that's hard to explain but impossible to ignore. Long watches, rough weather, close quarters, moments of humour in the middle of chaos – these shared experiences forge a connection that few other environments can match. That connection is called camaraderie, and if you're a leader, it's one of the most powerful tools at your disposal.

Camaraderie is more than just getting along. It's the trust that someone's got your back at 04:00 when you're soaked, tired and still pushing through. It's the quiet confidence that your team will pull together when things go sideways. And it's what keeps people focused, not because they're afraid of consequences, but because they don't want to let their teammates down.

As a leader, your job is to protect and nurture that bond. Camaraderie doesn't come from forced team-building or shallow incentives; it comes from shared effort, mutual respect and weathering challenges side by side. You don't need to be everyone's best mate, but you *do* need to adopt an environment where loyalty, humour and support can thrive.

Civilians sometimes underestimate this concept, thinking it's just a military thing. It's not. Camaraderie shows up in high-performing business teams, emergency services, classrooms and workshops. Wherever people are genuinely in it together, not just on paper, it builds stronger, faster, more resilient teams.

If you want a team that sticks together, communicates openly and performs under pressure, don't underestimate the quiet power of camaraderie. Build it, reinforce it and let it grow, and your leadership will be all the stronger for it.

3.7: Diversity and culture

Diversity isn't a leadership tick box; it's a strategic advantage. In the RN, I served alongside people from all walks of life: different backgrounds, faiths, accents, ages and skillsets. And I saw first hand that when these differences are valued and harnessed properly, they become a powerful force for innovation and operational success.

Strong teams are never made of clones. The best crews I worked with were a patchwork of experience and personality. But diversity alone is not enough. Inclusion is what turns that mix into a real team; it means people are heard, trusted and given the opportunity to lead.

As a leader, you set the tone. If you want a team that adapts quickly, solves problems creatively and respects one another, you must actively champion diversity, not just tolerate it. That means being intentional: listening widely, noticing when bias creeps in and lifting up those who might otherwise be overlooked.

It starts with something simple: everyone deserves a voice, not just the loudest, the most familiar or the highest in rank. Real inclusion means paying attention to who *isn't* speaking up. It means checking yourself when you instinctively lean on the same go-to people or make decisions based on comfort rather than merit. And when bias shows up, even in subtle ways, call it out professionally, but clearly.

The RN taught me to lead based on capability, not stereotype. I've seen quite junior rates outperform seasoned hands when given the chance, and I've seen diverse crews bond into high-functioning teams because everyone was treated with respect and fairness. The lesson? Talent doesn't come with a label and neither does leadership potential.

Every team also has its own culture, even within the same organisation. Whether you're on a ship, in a warehouse or running a project team, each group brings its own rhythms, values and unspoken rules. A good leader reads that culture, adapts where needed and helps shape it in a positive direction. That might mean rebalancing how decisions get made, making space for different communication styles or simply recognising that one size doesn't fit all.

Leadership in diverse teams takes effort. It requires self-awareness, emotional intelligence and the willingness to be uncomfortable now and then. But the payoff is massive: better teamwork, broader perspectives and stronger performance.

Inclusion doesn't just happen; it's led.

3.8: Earning loyalty through trust

I've already touched on micromanagement earlier in the book, so I won't labour the point here, but it's worth reinforcing one key idea: micromanagement is the enemy of trust. It often starts from a good place, a desire to keep things on track, avoid mistakes or ensure results. But however well intentioned, it sends a clear message: 'I don't trust you to handle this.'

If you catch yourself slipping into that mode, pause and ask yourself: is this about maintaining standards, or is it about control, fear or a lack of confidence in others or in yourself? Maybe someone let you down in the past. Maybe the pressure's piling on and you're trying to avoid failure. Whatever the reason, micromanagement chips away at morale. It creates anxious teams waiting for permission, not confident teams taking initiative.

Trust is the foundation of good leadership. And trust isn't handed out with rank; it's earned. Every time you delegate a task, listen properly, make a tough call or own a mistake, you're telling your team who you are as a leader. Get that right and they'll back you without hesitation. Get it wrong and they'll follow only because they must.

Loyalty doesn't come from pay packets or perks. It comes from consistency, fairness and shared purpose. If your team knows you've got their back, that you mean what you say and that you trust them to do their jobs, they'll repay that trust with everything they've got.

Leadership means building others up so they can lead too. The more trust you give, the more you'll earn. And when that trust matures into loyalty, your team becomes more than a group of individuals; it becomes a unit with heart.

Chapter 4

Leading by example

In leadership, actions speak louder than rank. You can't bluff credibility, and you certainly can't demand respect. You earn it. Whether you're on a warship or in an office, the most effective leaders are those who set the tone through their own behaviour.

Leading by example means showing up consistently, doing the hard things and holding yourself to the same, or higher, standard that you expect from your team. In the Royal Navy, this isn't optional. Your team watches what you do, how you react under pressure and how you handle responsibility. That tells them more about your leadership than any title or briefing ever could.

The same is true in any organisation. People don't just listen to what leaders say; they watch what they do. Your work ethic, your integrity, your attitude under pressure – that's what your team follows.

4.1: Walk the walk

Real respect doesn't come from a job title. Sure, people may admire a doctor or a judge for their position, but when you're leading a team, respect is earned through action, not authority.

One of the quickest ways to build that respect is simple: get stuck in.

There's nothing more reassuring to a team than seeing their leader roll up their sleeves and muck in with the everyday tasks. Watching a senior officer help bring fresh food stores on board? That sends a clear message: 'I'm with you. I'm part of this team.' And why shouldn't they help? They eat the same food as everyone else.

As a leader, you're not above the mundane. In fact, it's often those small, shared moments – making the brews, carrying a box, staying behind to sweep up – that earn you more respect than any rousing speech or command brief. It's leadership by example, and it builds something no inspection ever can: trust.

When your team sees that you're willing to walk the walk, not just talk the talk, they start to follow you by choice, not just by instruction. But walking the walk is more than just mucking in. It's also about living by the same standards you expect from everyone else. That's where consistency matters.

As engineers, we end up enforcing standards constantly, especially around personal protective equipment (PPE). And here's the truth: you can't preach safety and then wander into a machinery space without goggles or ear defenders. People notice. And the moment they see you cutting corners, they'll take that as permission to do the same.

I've lost count of the number of times I've had to stop someone heading into a space without the right kit or re-brief them during breathing apparatus preparation because they weren't wearing the correct PPE. You do not pull people up to be awkward, though some people seem to enjoy it. Most of the time, you do it to keep them safe, protect the people around them and protect yourself as well. And the only way anyone takes that seriously is if you take it seriously first.

That's walking the walk: not just doing the job, but being the standard.

4.2: The power of accountability

Leadership means owning your choices. Accountability means taking responsibility for the outcome, especially when things go wrong.

I've seen team leaders ignore procedures they've carried out 100 times. Familiarity breeds complacency, as the saying goes. And when mistakes happen, some are quick to point fingers – at machinery, at processes, at junior team members – anywhere but at themselves. But that's not leadership. In the Navy we call it sloping accountability, pushing the blame downhill instead of owning it and it's the fast track to losing respect.

As a leader, you must own it, whether the mistake is yours or your team's. I've stood in front of the CO and said, 'That's on me.' No excuses. No deflection.

Now, in the case I'm thinking of, it wasn't me who isolated the wrong system and flooded the wardroom; it was one of the lads having a brain fart and isolating the wrong one. When I asked what happened, he said he thought it was labelled backwards. I checked, and it was not, but it was clear he had simply got confused. I still took the hit for it. You would be surprised how much respect that earns, from above and below. When you take responsibility, you show strength. Sure, you might get a bollocking from higher up. But your team sees it, and more importantly, they remember it.

When you pass credit down the chain and take blame on the chin, you model something far more powerful than authority. You show what real accountability looks like and that builds loyalty, trust and a team that'll back you when it counts. (For more on accountability, see section 7.5.)

4.3: Ethical leadership

Ethics show up in the decisions no one sees. Whether it's enforcing standards fairly, dealing honestly with suppliers or refusing to take shortcuts, your integrity defines you more than any success story.

Take this example. During a maintenance period, a minor fault was discovered on a ship's fixed firefighting system. It wasn't a showstopper; on paper, the ship could've sailed. The fault was borderline, something that could have been logged, risk-assessed and waived with a bit of creative paperwork. And with the pressure of deadlines mounting, the temptation was real: tick the box, move on, keep the schedule. But the senior engineer in charge made the call: 'Fix it properly.'

That choice meant several days of delay and a full work-up of the system – not popular, not convenient, but right.

When the ship eventually sailed, it was fully compliant, safe and ready for anything. More importantly, the crew sailed with a clear message: doing the right thing isn't optional, it's the standard.

That decision did more than fix a fault. It reinforced a culture. It showed that leadership is built on integrity, especially when no one is watching, not speed or ticking boxes. That is ethical leadership in action. And it is how you earn respect that lasts long after the paperwork has been signed.

4.4: Look the part

On board, we lived and breathed standards, from how we wore our kit to the way we kept our workspaces squared away. Looking the part wasn't about vanity – it was about discipline, mindset and pride in what we represented.

In civilian leadership, that principle still applies. You do not need to be flashy; you need to be sharp, composed and able to set the tone for others. Your presentation, your dress, your posture, even how you speak, sends a message long before you open your mouth.

Whether you're showing up to a meeting prepared, delivering clear instructions or just carrying yourself with purpose, people will mirror your energy. If you look as if you've got your act together, it builds confidence in those around you. If you're sloppy, dishevelled or disinterested, don't be surprised if your team starts to reflect the same.

What's the old saying? If you look good, you feel good. But more importantly, if you look ready, people trust that you are. Leadership starts with presence. Show up like it matters, because it does.

4.5: Confidence

Confidence isn't arrogance, although there is a fine line between the two. It does not come from being the loudest voice in the room or pretending to know everything. It's the steady tone you hold when things get tense. It's the ability to pause instead of panic. It's saying 'I don't know, but I'll find out' when you're caught off guard and owning that without shame.

The most confident leaders I've served with didn't shout. They didn't strut. They asked good questions. They listened closely. And when the moment came, they made clear, decisive calls without fuss. That quiet blend of humility and poise is what teams rally behind.

Remember: we're all human. We all make mistakes.

True confidence comes from moving through it. It's knowing that failure doesn't define you and that showing vulnerability doesn't make you weak. It makes you relatable. Approachable. *Real.*

Confidence is built through competence, repetition and self-awareness, not bravado. You don't need to be bulletproof. You just need to be dependable under pressure.

That's what earns trust. That's what sets a leader apart.

4.6: Servant leadership

Servant leadership means putting the team first. Simple as that. It's the officer who quietly stays back after a long day to help a JR revise for a promotion board. It's the shift supervisor who jumps into the night rota when a team member's dealing with a family emergency, not for recognition, but because it's the right thing to do.

It's the manager who listens more than they talk, who advocates for development opportunities, and who steps in to shoulder the load when their team's struggling. Servant leaders don't see people as resources; they see them as people.

When done right, servant leadership builds trust, loyalty and long-term performance. It tells your team: 'I see you. I've got your back.'

But be aware, some people will try to use it against you. If you're always stepping in, always carrying the load, a few may start expecting it. They'll rely on your support instead of owning their responsibilities. So, serve your team, but don't become a servant.

The part people often get wrong with servant leadership is that it doesn't mean being passive or avoiding difficult conversations. In fact, if you genuinely care about your people and the team, you can't afford to let problems slide just to keep the peace. Letting poor attitude, resentment or low-level friction fester isn't kindness – it's neglect.

Real servant leadership lifts others up, but it also teaches them to stand on their own. And sometimes leading by example means dealing with people head on, not just fixing problems or stepping into the rota.

If someone's got an attitude, I don't dance around it. I ask them straight: 'What's the problem?' Nine times out of ten, once it's out in the open, you find it's not defiance, it's stress, confusion or something going on outside work. Getting it on the table means you can deal with it before it festers.

4.7: Problem solving under pressure

Whether we realise it or not, we solve problems every day. From managing last-minute changes to handling unexpected issues, problem solving is a constant part of life and leadership. But the *pressure* we feel when doing it? That's shaped by a range of factors. It could be time constraints. It could be safety risks. It could be the people watching, the resources on the line or just the fear of getting it wrong.

When you're leading a team under pressure, the problem is only part of what matters; it's your *response* to it. And that response is driven by mindset.

Pressure doesn't create poor decisions. *Mindset under pressure* does.

Some freeze. Some react emotionally. Others focus, breathe and lead through it, calmly, methodically and with intent. That's not about being superhuman. It's about training your brain to treat pressure as a prompt, not a panic.

Strong leaders bring stability when things go sideways. They don't need to know all the answers, but they know how to slow things down, ask the right questions and move forward without feeding the chaos.

Because under pressure, your team isn't just watching the outcome.

They're watching *you.*

4.8: Lead as if they're watching

Because they are. Your team is always watching. Not to judge, though some will – that's human nature – but to learn. They learn how to lead by watching you. They watch how you handle pressure. How you treat people. How you show up when it's hard and no one would blame you for ducking out.

Having a fancy title and giving speeches does not make you a great leader. Showing up and setting the tone, day in, day out.

Owning the outcome. Walking the walk. Whether you're sailing a ship or driving projects on land, lead in a way that earns more than just compliance – lead in a way that earns loyalty.

Ask yourself:

- ⚓ Do I do what I ask others to do?
- ⚓ Do I take responsibility, publicly, when things go wrong?
- ⚓ Do I set a standard I'd be proud for others to follow?

If the answer is yes, then you're not just leading – you're leading by example. People copy what you do, not what you say. And that's exactly why how you apply pressure matters. When people are watching you for cues, they're not just listening to your words; they're absorbing your behaviour. How you correct, challenge or push matters just as much as what you're asking for.

If you drop your standards, they'll drop theirs. And if you have to shout to get people to act, that's not leadership, that's a loss of control. Shouting might get short-term movement, but it teaches the wrong lesson. It tells people that volume equals authority, and that pressure replaces trust. Respect is earned by how you carry yourself, especially in the moments where you're tempted to snap.

Chapter 5

Tools in your arsenal

Leadership takes more than presence and intuition; it also requires the right tools at the right time. Whether you're planning ahead, motivating your team, making tough calls or steering through change, practical frameworks can give you clarity and structure when it matters most.

In this chapter, I'll walk you through the tools I've used myself, from engine rooms to boardrooms. These aren't academic theories. They're real-world methods I've relied on under pressure, and you'll find each one explained simply, with examples. You'll also find printable versions in the appendices, ready to adapt to your own leadership context.

Whether you're setting team goals, making decisions or reflecting after a crisis, grab the tool that fits and crack on.

5.1: Strategic planning tools

These are the frameworks that help you get ahead of the game. Whether you're mapping a mission, scoping a project or tackling an operational challenge, these tools help you break the task down, set priorities and focus your team.

SWOT it

The SWOT analysis helps you quickly assess any situation by identifying:

SWOT analysis	
Strengths	*What are we good at? What resources, skills or advantages do we have?*
Weaknesses	*What can we improve? What limitations or challenges do we face?*
Opportunities	*What external factors or resources can we use to succeed?*
Threats	*What external risks or obstacles could hinder our success?*

This tool is ideal for planning team projects, assessing readiness, or prepping for reviews. It brings clarity and helps you make better-informed decisions. (See **Appendix B** for a completed example.)

SMART thinking

Goals without structure often fail. SMART objectives keep you and your team on track:

SMART objectives	
Specific	*Define what you want to achieve. Explain: Who? What? Where? Why?*
Measurable	*Make sure everyone understands how a successful outcome will be achieved.*
Achievable	*Break down goals into smaller, manageable tasks, avoid overloading the team.*
Relevant	*The goal should contribute meaningfully to the team's mission or vision.*
Time-bound	*Set a realistic, motivating deadline that creates urgency without causing stress while maintaining accountability.*

Use SMART when defining any key output or when giving team direction. (See **Appendix C** for how to draft one).

Objectives need key results (OKRs)

OKRs are a powerful way to keep a team aligned:

Objective	Key results
Set a clear, to the point and inspiring goal that everyone within your team understands and can work towards.	*KRs should be specific, showing exactly how success will be measured.*
	Stay organised, tick them off as you complete them.
	KRs should align with the broader goal of the objective following a logical order (eg KR1, KR2, KR3).
	Defined KRs will keep the team focused on what matters most.
	KRs should state every team member's role and responsibilities, ensuring they are accountable.

They work well in high-stakes or fast-paced environments where you need to break down bigger missions into bite-sized, trackable chunks.

5.2: Task management and workflow tools

These tools prevent the dreaded 'Who's doing what?' confusion. They clarify roles, simplify tasking and reduce inefficiency.

RACI Matrix

This tool helps everyone understand their role on a task:

RACI Matrix	
Responsible	*The person who does the job.*
Accountable	*The person who makes sure the job gets done.*
Consulted	*People who give advice or input before the task is done.*
Informed	*People who need updates on the task but don't actively work on it.*

Used right, a RACI Matrix (PMI 2000) avoids crossed wires, task duplication and 'not my job' excuses.

The Eisenhower Matrix

This matrix helps leaders prioritise tasks by sorting them into:

	Urgent	Not urgent
Important	**Do first** *Tasks that need immediate attention and have significant consequences if delayed.*	**Schedule** *Tasks that are crucial for long-term goals but don't require immediate action.*
Not important	**Delegate** *Tasks that need quick action but can be handled by others.*	**Eliminate** *Tasks that offer little value and can be removed to save time.*

Use this when you're overloaded or trying to help your team work smarter. (**Appendix D** shows how to apply it to event planning.)

5.3: Team collaboration tools

In both civilian workplaces and the Navy, strong communication and team rhythm make or break performance. These tools help build that rhythm.

Have a daily stand-up

Short, focused and held at the same time daily. The aim? Align the team, surface issues and keep people accountable.

Before leading a stand-up:

- ⚓ Prepare a brief plan of action.
- ⚓ Give your update clearly.
- ⚓ Ask: 'Any blockers?' or 'Does everyone know their role?'

They're used daily across the RN and work equally well in fast-paced civilian teams.

Give some SBI feedback

The SBI model from the Center for Creative Leadership makes feedback clear and constructive:

SBI feedback model	
Situation	*Describe when and where the event took place.*
Behaviour	*Explain what the person did.*
Impact	*Describe how their actions affected the team or mission.*

Use this to coach, correct or praise without causing embarrassment or frustration.

5.4: Continual improvement tools

Leadership also means evolving yourself and your team. These tools are about reflection, learning and doing better next time.

Using Driscoll's model of reflection

Ask three simple questions after any experience (Driscoll 2007):

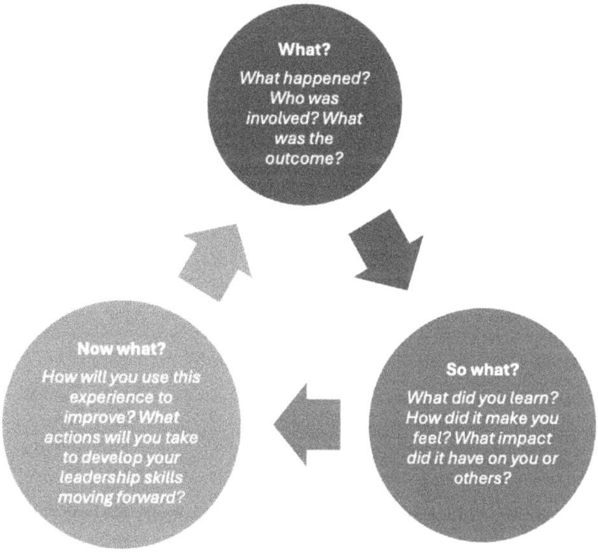

Great for reviewing an incident, project or meeting. It promotes honest self-assessment. (Explore this further in **Appendix G**.)

A continuous PDCA cycle

Plan–Do–Check–Act is a go-to process for improving workflows or fixing recurring issues:

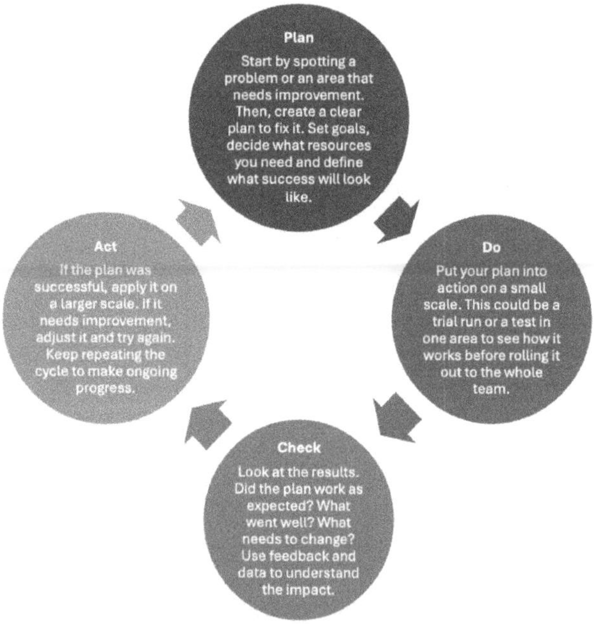

This is how high-functioning teams build momentum and get better over time.

5.5: Motivation: push vs pull leadership

One thing you learn quickly as a leader, especially in the Navy, is that people do not move just because you tell them to. They move because they understand why it matters. That is the difference between pushing your team and pulling them with you.

Push leadership is when you drive things with pressure, deadlines, orders, raised voices and urgency. It works, but only in short bursts.

Pull leadership is when people step up because they believe in the job, feel trusted and understand the bigger picture. That is where long-term motivation comes from.

Here is an example. We were alongside Dubai, second day in.

It was a working day, and at 08:00 a pipe went out: 'Clear lower deck, store ship.' That meant the whole ship's company was to form a line from the jetty, across the gangway, through the ship and down to the main food stores to bring on fresh provisions. It is a tedious but necessary job.

A lot of the JRs had gone out the night before. It was their first time in Dubai, excitement was high, and one lad turned up looking rough – late, dehydrated and clearly regretting his choices. I watched from a distance as his chain of command reacted in two completely different ways.

His PO went straight for the push. He hammered him for turning up late, looking like death and not being fit for work. None of it was wrong. The lad had stitched himself up and we all knew it. But the more the PO laid into him, the slower he became. Shoulders down, brain off, just surviving the rollocking. Classic compliance but zero motivation.

His killick took a different tack. Quiet voice, no drama. 'Come on mate, dig out for half an hour, get this done, and you can crash out at lunchtime. Let's just get the ship stored.'

That was the pull. A bit of understanding, a bit of direction and a clear reason to put the effort in. And instantly the lad moved better. Not perfect, but faster, sharper, switched back on. Because someone talked to him like a human being, not a problem.

Two leaders, same sailor, totally different results. Motivation is rarely about volume – it is about approach.

Before we get into the detail, here are a few simple distinctions that explain why some approaches work better than others when you are trying to motivate people, whether at sea or ashore.

- ⚓ **Extrinsic vs intrinsic motivation:** Push motivates from outside through pressure and consequences. Pull motivates from inside through pride, purpose and belonging. One fades quickly; the other lasts.
- ⚓ **Military vs civilian motivation:** In the Navy, people will push through difficult conditions for the person next to them. In civilian teams, people push harder when they feel heard and involved.
  Different triggers, same human need: purpose and respect.

The three things leaders tend to get wrong about motivation are:

1. They shout instead of explain.
2. They assume everyone is motivated the same way.
3. They forget people follow tone, not volume.

Pull more than you push. Pressure gets compliance. Purpose gets commitment.

Chapter 6

Decision making

Good decision making is a bit like being a chef preparing a critical meal for a hungry crew on the high seas. You've got limited time, high expectations, unpredictable conditions and no room for mistakes. Whether you're leading in a kitchen, a control room or a boardroom, the pressure to make the right call and make it fast is real.

Decision making isn't a one-size-fits-all process. In the Navy, I had to make calm, time-critical calls while machinery failed or chaos kicked off around me. But in civilian life, decisions still carry weight: hiring, risk, budget and people.

This chapter introduces tested leadership frameworks that help you make better decisions, faster. These aren't just theories; they're proven tools I've relied on at sea and now use with business clients across industries. From staying calm in a crisis to cutting through ambiguity, you'll find methods that support clear, confident leadership. (See Appendices.)

This chapter explores how to stay sharp under pressure, cut through uncertainty and lead with clarity when it counts most.

6.1: Staying calm in a storm

There comes a moment in every leader's journey when all eyes turn to them and the clock starts ticking. Something fails. A plan unravels. An unexpected problem lands in your lap. In that moment, you're expected to act quickly, think clearly and stay composed.

In the RN, those moments were routine. Systems failed mid-mission. Weather turned without warning. Orders changed overnight. The margin for error was small, and hesitation could cost time, credibility or lives.

The leaders who stood out weren't the loudest or the most experienced. They were the ones who stayed calm in the storm. They prepared well, trusted their people and knew how to slow the moment down when everything else sped up.

I saw this clearly on one ship where our MEO and DMEO simply did not get along.

On paper, they were meant to be a united leadership team. In reality, there was constant friction. The DMEO would make quiet digs and issue conflicting direction. The MEO never reacted publicly. He stayed professional, but the lack of alignment filtered straight down into the department. The result was confusion, tension and people being pulled in different directions depending on who spoke to them last.

One morning it came to a head. Within minutes, I received two completely different sets of instructions – something not uncommon at the time.

The MEO's direction was clear and sensible: secure the engine spaces and get the department ready to sail. It was operationally sound and time critical.

Shortly after, the DMEO appeared and insisted we drop everything to help him. His job wasn't urgent. It wasn't essential. It felt like point scoring – senior egos clashing, with the department caught in the middle. Either way, someone was going to be unhappy.

So I slowed it down and went back to basics. Who holds accountability? Who signs off the department's output? The answer was clear: the MEO.

I briefed the team: 'We'll do what the MEO wants first. Once that's done, we will give the DMEO a hand. If there's an issue, or he moans at you let me know and I will speak to him.'

We cracked on.

Later, the MEO thanked the lads. The DMEO knew exactly what he'd tried to do. One led with professionalism. The other led with ego.

When senior leaders can't agree, someone below them still has to stay steady. If they don't, the whole department starts to sink. That's not easy, especially in a toxic environment, but your job isn't to get dragged into other people's battles. Your job is to protect your team and make decisions that serve the mission, not the noise.

That same mindset applies in civilian leadership. You might not face fires or flooding, but you *will* face market shocks, staffing crises, product failures and legal pressure. When that happens, how you respond under pressure is what defines you as a leader.

6.2: Decision making and problem solving

Good decisions come from good thinking, and good thinking starts with clarity under pressure. That doesn't mean you always have the full picture. Often, especially in the Navy, you don't. But even when information is limited, you still need a process to guide you through.

Listen like a leader

Under stress, poor leaders react. Good leaders listen first: to the environment, their team and their own instincts. Listening doesn't slow you down – it sharpens your thinking. You spot what others miss, catch inconsistencies early and create space for better input from the people who actually know the problem.

I remember a fault on one platform where two of my lads were arguing about the cause. One was convinced it was an electrical issue. The other was adamant there was a mechanical blockage. Instead of shutting one down or picking a side, I got them both to explain their thinking properly. Not just what they thought the problem was, but *why*.

What became clear was this: both of them had a valid point. An electrical short had triggered a mechanical issue. If I'd dismissed one view in favour of the other, we'd have wasted hours chasing the wrong fix and probably caused a fair bit of friction in the process.

Remember, listening doesn't mean indecision.

At the end of the day, the call was still mine to make. I laid it out clearly: 'We'll try it this way first. If that doesn't fix it, we move straight to plan B.' That way, everyone knew the plan, everyone knew there was an alternative plan and everyone felt heard.

That matters. When you shut people down, they stop contributing. When you listen properly, even if you don't follow their suggestion, they stay engaged because they know their input counts.

In high-pressure environments, people shut down fast when they feel ignored. If you want honest insight from your team when it really matters, start by making listening part of how you lead every day, not just when things go wrong.

6.3: High-stakes decisions

When there's no time for meetings or deep analysis, a simplified version of the Navy's operational planning mindset can help. Here's a quick framework:

Five-step decision-making approach:

Step	Description
1. Orient to reality	What's happening? Strip away assumptions and rumours. Get to the facts, fast.
2. Prioritise outcomes	What matters most right now? Safety? Time? Budget? Morale? Decide what you're optimising for.
3. Scan for resources	What tools, people or information do you have access to immediately?
4. Act decisively	Choose a course. Communicate clearly. Own the decision.
5. Adapt fast	Watch what happens. Be ready to pivot. Adjust as soon as new information becomes available.

This way of thinking isn't theoretical. It's exactly how decisions are made in real-world, high-threat environments.

In recent years, RN ships have been operating in areas where the threat is real, fast-moving and often ambiguous. In places like the Red Sea, threats haven't always come in traditional forms. Cheap, widely available systems like drones mean danger and can appear suddenly, with very little warning. Leaders often have seconds, not minutes, to decide how to respond.

When a potential threat is detected, alarms sound, reports flood in and information arrives in incomplete and sometimes contradictory forms. Is it a confirmed hostile contact or a false track? Is it one system or several? Is the priority defence, manoeuvre or communication up the chain? There's no time for lengthy discussion. People are looking to their leaders to make sense of the chaos.

What stands out to me in those environments isn't aggressive decision making, but calm decision making. The most effective leaders don't panic or rush to impress. They slow the moment down mentally, prioritise what matters most (usually safety and containment) and act decisively with the information available, adjusting as the situation unfolds.

That's the real value of a repeatable decision-making framework under pressure. It stops fear and noise from driving the response and allows leaders to think clearly when it matters most.

The same principle applies outside the military. You may never face a drone swarm, but you *will* face fast-moving crises, incomplete information and high-consequence decisions. The leaders who perform best aren't the ones who wait for certainty; they're the ones who can think clearly, decide calmly and adapt quickly when the situation changes.

6.4: Uncertain and ambiguous situations

Some of the hardest leadership decisions happen in the grey zone, where there's no clear answer, no complete data and no time to wait. In military operations, that's normal. You act with incomplete intelligence, shifting conditions and changing objectives. You don't get the luxury of perfect information. Over time, that builds resilience and adaptability in a leader.

Everyone in the Navy is trained to fight fires. And while they're dangerous, they're fought in an environment we know. A sailor understands the layout of their ship. They know the compartments, the access routes and, more importantly, the escape routes. Even in chaos, there's a mental map to work from.

That's why I've always had huge respect for civilian fire-fighters. Every fire they turn up to is different: different building, different layout, hidden dangers, unknown materials, poor visibility and often incomplete or unreliable information. They might get a quick brief on the way in, but once they commit to entry, conditions can change rapidly and assumptions fall away.

Intelligence is critical. You want as much information as possible. What's inside. Who's inside. Where the risks are. But when someone's trapped, time is against you. Waiting for perfect information isn't an option.

When seconds matter, the most crucial information required is simple:

- What is happening?
- Where is it happening?
- What has already been done?
- Are there any casualties?

No waffle. No backstory. Just the essentials needed to act.

For example: 'There's a carbonaceous fire, port side forward, in the ship's office. I attacked it with one foam fire extinguisher but was beaten back. The door to the compartment has been shut. No casualties within the space.'

That single snapshot gives a leader enough clarity to make decisions, allocate resources and stay ahead of the situation, even though the full picture is still forming.

The principle carries straight across into leadership. You make decisions with what you have, not what you wish you had. You balance risk, urgency and responsibility. You give clear direction, even when the situation itself is unclear.

It also means the person in charge of the firefighting team preparing to re-enter the compartment can be clear and upfront with their team, without panicking:

'Here's what we know. Here's what we don't know. Here's what we're doing next.'

You don't need perfect information to lead people. You just need enough clarity to keep them moving, and enough calm to stop uncertainty turning into paralysis.

That's leadership in the grey zone – not certainty, not control, just direction, honesty and the confidence to act when time won't wait.

6.5: Competing priorities

If you want a proper lesson in competing priorities, look at damage control.

Damage control is everything a ship's company does to keep the ship afloat, fighting and alive after something has gone wrong: fires, flooding, battle damage, system failures. It's about containing the problem, protecting people and preserving the ship's ability to fight on. Everyone on board is trained for it, because when it happens, there's no time to wait for specialists.

Earlier in the book I said that when we're not at war, the priority on board is people. Safety first, no argument. That principle holds true in normal operations, exercises and peacetime routines.

But in war, or when a ship takes serious damage, the priorities get messy very quickly. Because sometimes protecting people in the immediate moment clashes with protecting the ship itself. And if the ship goes, everyone ends up in the water.

Flooding is a good example. If a compartment is taking water and you can't stop it, you might be forced to shut the hatch, isolate the space and accept that you've 'lost' it. It's a horrible decision, but it can be survivable. Ships are built with compartmentation for exactly this reason: to contain damage and stay afloat even when parts of the ship are sacrificed.

Fire is different. Flooding can often be contained. Fire spreads. Smoke spreads. Heat migrates. Systems fail. And once fire gets ahead of you, you're no longer fighting a fire; you're fighting for the ship.

Both are damage control situations, but the risks and priorities are different. That's why damage control is drilled into everyone, and why the real aim is always the same: contain and control the damage, minimise casualties and preserve the ship's ability to keep operating.

Leadership in those moments becomes triage. Deciding what matters most right now.

- Do we commit people to re-enter, or do we pull back and change the plan?
- Do we isolate a space and write it off, or do we gamble to save it?

- ⚓ Do we prioritise life-saving, stability or getting capability back online?

And you have to make those calls knowing not everyone will agree with you. That's the job.

A ship's captain doesn't make these decisions alone. They rely on information fed up from their immediate team: the warfare officer, the marine engineer officer, the navigator and others. Each department sees the situation through its own lens. Warfare wants to keep fighting. Engineers want power, propulsion and systems online. Command want clarity: what's happening, what's changed and which options are still on the table.

The captain's role is to pull all of that information together, see the bigger picture and decide what takes priority *now*. The quality of that decision depends entirely on how clearly and honestly information is passed up through the chain.

Outside the Navy, leadership in these moments means refusing to take sides. It's the same triage mindset as damage control, just without the smoke. You balance priorities, protect safety and timelines, keep diplomacy intact and make it clear that the mission comes before egos.

Be fair. Be firm. And above all, don't take nonsense from people who confuse arrogance with importance.

Chapter 7

Discipline and resilience

Discipline = success. In the RN, discipline isn't optional; it's embedded in everything we do. It shapes how we train, how we show up, how we execute under pressure and ultimately, how we succeed. Without discipline, even the best plans fall apart. With it, teams stay sharp, focused and effective, no matter what comes their way.

Discipline means consistency, standards and accountability, all of which build trust and drive performance. It is not punishment or control, despite what many people assume. Whether you're leading a team through intense operational pressure or sustaining momentum across a long deployment, disciplined leadership creates clarity: people know what to expect, what's expected of them and that there are no shortcuts.

You might be tempted to associate discipline only with combat scenarios, but that's not the full story. In truth, discipline shows its value in quieter moments: keeping a team on track during routine maintenance, maintaining standards during back-to-back night watches or staying focused when everyone's counting the days to home port. In these moments, it's the leader's consistency that holds everything together.

The same principles apply in civilian organisations. A disciplined team hits its targets. A disciplined leader keeps things moving, even when it's awkward, inconvenient or tough to explain. Over time, that discipline becomes part of the culture – one that values precision, follow through and doing things properly, not just quickly.

7.1: Bouncing back from failure

Setbacks are part of leadership. Missions don't always go to plan. Systems fail. Comms go down. Sometimes, you make the wrong call.

In the Navy, failure isn't the end, but it is always examined. Every mistake is an opportunity to reflect, adjust and reapply. There's no time for endless finger pointing or sulking. You figure out what went wrong, own what you can and crack on.

Now, let's be honest, there's *always* someone who'll try to deflect blame (affectionately known as 'shit deflector'). But not everyone is built to lead. Some duck responsibility. You don't. That's what sets you apart.

This mindset builds resilience. And resilient teams don't fall apart under pressure; they recalibrate and carry on.

In civilian life, the same attitude separates good leaders from great ones. When things go off track, be it a failed pitch, a lost client or a tech disaster, resilient leaders step up. They take accountability, hold the team together and focus on recovery, not excuses.

Failure kicks you in the teeth sometimes, but if you're switched on, you'll learn faster and come back stronger.

Want to go deeper into leading through chaos? See Chapter 17.3 on leadership in uncertainty.

7.2: Self-discipline

You can't lead others if you can't lead yourself. In the military, which started with routine, timekeeping, personal presentation and mental readiness, it extended to how you prepared for tasks, how you treated others and how you showed up in high-pressure moments.

Self-discipline is the foundation of credibility. If you don't follow through on your own expectations, why should your team follow you?

In civilian life, that shows up in a hundred small, visible ways:

⚓ **Meeting your own deadlines**: You don't miss meetings, show up late or leave work unfinished. If you ask for urgency from others, your own delivery must be on point first.

- **Managing your emotions**: When things go sideways, whether it's a client complaint or a blown budget, you stay steady – no flapping or finger pointing, just calm leadership that reassures the team.
- **Staying prepared and proactive**: You show up ready. Whether it's a Monday morning briefing or a crisis response meeting, you've done the prep and thought through the next step before being asked.
- **Avoiding blame culture**: You take ownership when things go wrong. Not because it's fun, but because it's fair. That honesty earns trust far quicker than throwing others under the bus.
- **Practising what you preach**: If you talk about work–life balance, you model it. If you say quality matters, you double-check your own output. People watch what you *do* far more than what you say.

Disciplined leaders lead from the front – not by shouting louder, but by quietly setting the example, day in and day out. That consistency speaks louder than any motivational speech.

7.3: Managing stress

Leadership under pressure demands emotional control. Stress is guaranteed. What matters is how you respond to it and how you help your team stay focused through it.

In the Navy, you are deliberately trained in conditions that are wet, cold, sleep-depriving, uncomfortable and uncertain. You may find yourself launching a sea boat in freezing rain at three in the morning, running a damage control exercise after a full day's work or dealing with a machinery defect when you're already exhausted.

None of it is accidental. It is deliberate conditioning, teaching you to function when your body and emotions are under strain. Because in a real emergency, panic does not help. You acknowledge the stress, you contain it and you keep going. You breathe. You prioritise. And you lead.

That same principle applies in civilian leadership. The pressure may look different: deadlines, budgets, customer complaints, constant change – but the emotional load is just as real. Teams don't expect their leader to be stress free; they expect them to be steady.

Don't pretend stress isn't there and don't glorify suffering either. Normalise it. Stress is something to work with, not something to hide or silently endure.

Decades of psychological and medical research (McEwen 2007; Maslach & Leiter 2016) show what happens when stress has nowhere to go. Leaders who bottle it up don't suddenly explode in dramatic fashion. It comes out in smaller, more damaging ways: snapping at people, poor judgement, tunnel vision, over-controlling details or quietly disengaging. Psychologists have been pointing out for years that unrelieved stress impairs decision making, narrows thinking and increases the likelihood of burnout and mistakes. Teams usually feel the impact long before the leader realises what's happening.

Handled properly, exposure to pressure builds capability. Like physical training, leadership under stress only strengthens you when it's deliberate, controlled and followed by recovery and reflection. Constant overload without release doesn't build resilience; it grinds people down (trust me, I know).

But – and this is a big but – you must find healthy outlets. In the old days of the Navy, stress relief often meant consuming alcohol, and lots of it. It was the default pressure valve, and for many it caused long-term damage. That mindset has changed. Today, de-stressing looks more like fitness, journaling, talking things through, getting outdoors or simply switching off your phone and spending time with the people who keep you grounded. Find what works for you and protect it.

Stress is part of leadership. Burnout, breakdowns and bad calls don't come from pressure alone. They come from pressure that's ignored or never released. So, lead by example. Don't just manage your team's output; model how to manage pressure properly as well.

7.4: Balancing empowerment and authority

Discipline doesn't mean dictatorship. Some of the best leaders I've served under knew how to strike a balance between firm authority and genuine empowerment. They didn't micromanage every move, but they weren't afraid to take charge when it mattered either. They knew when to direct and when to delegate. And above all, they trusted the team to step up when it counted.

Delegation means more than just sloping off jobs; it's leadership in action. Yes, you're assigning responsibility, but you're also giving context, setting expectations and letting people take ownership inside a clear framework. You don't just say 'crack on'. You say: 'Here's the why, here's the standard and here's where you've got room to own it.' (If the thought of delegating tasks makes you uncomfortable, check out **Appendix G: Delegation tips**.)

Empowered teams don't just get more done. They think more creatively. They take pride in their work. And when something goes wrong, they don't point fingers, they fix it.

But let's not get it twisted: empowerment doesn't mean a free-for-all. Even the most capable teams still need leadership. That means:

- ⚓ **Set the standards**: Make it clear what good looks like, with no ambiguity.
- ⚓ **Stay available**: Give support, not interference. Be there when needed, not hovering.
- ⚓ **Make the hard calls**: When things go grey, the leader decides. Full stop.

It's not a question of authority or trust – it's both. Clarity gives direction. Trust gives momentum. You lead best when you offer both.

7.5: Accountability

Whether you're navigating extreme depths aboard a nuclear submarine, standing on the deck of an aircraft carrier overseeing the launch and recovery of fighter jets or patrolling the coastline to protect the nation's fisheries, one truth remains the same: accountability matters. In fact, it can be the difference between mission success and catastrophic failure.

In the RN, the smallest lapse in accountability can trigger a chain reaction: a missed valve check, an incorrect fuel reading or a delayed command. Any one of these can endanger lives, disable systems or compromise an entire operation. That's why leadership at sea doesn't give you room to dodge accountability;

you get a moment to sort yourself out, then own it. No excuses, no 'it wasn't me'. If it happened on your watch, it's yours to own.

That mindset applies directly to civilian life, especially in roles where compliance, safety and precision are critical.

A shift manager at Wetherspoons isn't just there to check timesheets. They're responsible for ensuring food hygiene is up to spec, customers are safe and sober, and the team is performing professionally. If something goes wrong – an injury, a service failure, a serious complaint – it reflects on the leader, not just the individual.

In the NHS, a single overlooked entry in a patient's chart can result in misdiagnosis or mistreatment. And while it might be a junior member who makes the error, the ultimate responsibility lies with the leadership team: the charge nurse, the ward manager, the department lead. It's their job to create clarity, maintain standards and own the outcome.

The same applies in construction, logistics, finance, education, you name it. In every environment where people, safety or livelihoods are on the line, accountability is a duty, not just a process.

A strong accountability culture sharpens the team. It removes grey areas and builds trust and pride. It sends a message: we don't cut corners here. And it always starts with you.

And here's something worth remembering: accountability is closely tied to personal pride. Effective leaders don't hide when things go wrong – they step up. They say, 'That's on me.' Not because they're looking to be the hero, but because they understand that leadership without ownership is just noise.

When your team sees you take responsibility, especially in the hard moments, they're far more likely to do the same. That's how a culture of excellence is built: from the top down, and by example.

Accountability isn't a burden; it's a badge of honour. Wear it well.

7.6: Emotional resilience

Mental toughness means staying steady, showing calm under pressure, optimism during setbacks and strength under scrutiny, even when you're running on empty.

Your emotional state sets the tone for your team. They take cues from how you carry yourself. If you're angry, flustered or disengaged, they'll mirror it. But if you're composed, fair and consistent, even chaos feels manageable. This doesn't mean faking it. Resilience doesn't mean being a robot. It means knowing how to hold the space and when to recharge before you break.

You're not there to be perfect. You're there to be predictable.

If you're leading while burned out, or trying to support someone else who's struggling, Chapter 17 covers both with more depth and honesty than I could squeeze in here.

Discipline and resilience aren't just traits, they're habits. Practised daily, they shape how you lead, how your team performs and how your culture grows.

Ask yourself:

- Do I lead with consistency, even when no one's watching?
- Do I bounce back quickly when plans go off course?
- Do I model calm, clarity and control, especially under pressure?

If so, you're not just managing – you're leading with backbone.

Chapter 8

Adaptive leadership

There's one quality that separates decent leaders from great ones: adaptability. Plans are nice until the world decides otherwise. At sea, you learn fast that the weather doesn't give a toss about your intentions. One minute the sea is calm, the next you're grabbing a guard rail as a wave hits out of nowhere. A skilled sailor spots the shift early and braces for the storm; a skilled leader does exactly the same.

Adaptability isn't some leadership buzzword. It's that mix of frustration turning into focus, excitement edging into adrenaline and the outward calm you try to project even when, deep down, you're thinking, 'Damn, here we go again...' Things change fast, and your team will watch how you respond.

What matters isn't whether the situation stays stable; it won't. What matters is whether you can pivot without losing your composure or your people.

Darwin suggested that survival comes down to adaptability, not strength. In leadership, that's not just survival – it's your superpower.

8.1: Why adaptability is non-negotiable

Picture the scene. We were halfway through a replenishment at sea (RAS) in the North Sea, a vital but hazardous operation where fuel is transferred from a logistics ship to a warship while both are underway. That day, the weather turned fast.

I was down in the forward generator room, standing on the

fuelling trunk, directing fuel into the forward tanks while my opposite number handled the aft. Even down there, warm and dry, the ship started rolling enough to make you brace at every step. And I remember thinking: 'Thank God I'm not one of the poor sods on the upper deck getting battered by the wind and rain.'

Then the signs started. The weather was shifting more quickly than the forecast, and you could feel it in everything. Voices on the comms got shorter and more clipped as people focused on conditions getting sketchy. I could hear the sea battering the hull, so God knows how rough it was getting topside.

The vibe went from routine to 'hang on... this isn't right'. The crane crew on the logistics ship shut down instantly. Comms between the two ships started dropping out. The sea state had risen so fast that carrying on would've been downright dangerous. RAS gear and heavy lines don't forgive mistakes when the ship's being thrown around. One wrong move and someone pays for it.

So that was it – operation over. And we were left with only part of the fuel we needed.

Low fuel. Rising sea state. No safe way to continue.

In peacetime, you don't risk lives for diesel. If this had been wartime, it would have been a different story. You'd probably press on because running out of fuel is its own kind of suicide. But on a Tuesday in the North Sea? The right call is the safe call. That's adaptability: recognising that the moment has changed and adjusting before the situation decides for you. And that's exactly what happened. A joint call between the captains of both ships.

Our CO knew we needed the fuel, but he also knew the risks were now unacceptable. So he looked to his team, in this case the MEO, for options. Between them they didn't waste a second. The MEO already had a Plan B forming. Systems were reprioritised, a revised fuel usage plan was put together and everyone who needed to know got the message: conserve fuel, adjust routines and operate under the new restrictions: clear, calm and controlled.

My standout memory is just trying to stay upright while the deck bucked beneath me, cracking on with my job while the storm made itself known, even below decks. But the tone was set from the top, and that's what kept everything steady.

What I took from that day is simple: adaptability isn't failing, it's awareness. It's calling it how it is, changing course when the facts change and not pretending you're bulletproof just because you're in uniform. You don't lose credibility by adapting; you lose it by ignoring reality.

Whether you're in uniform or in civvies, afloat or ashore, adaptability isn't optional. It's what separates leaders from passengers.

8.2: Flexibility in action

The best example I can give you of staying flexible was when I was on board a certain destroyer. We had spent months working up for a deployment to the Arabian Gulf. That meant all our kit and equipment was checked, heat-proofed and ready. The warfare department were running anti-swarm drills, boarding exercises and layered defence training, all geared towards operating off the coast of a particularly unfriendly country (you know the one).

We were preparing to escort high-value merchant vessels through the Strait of Hormuz, where tensions can flare fast and the temperatures can hit 50°C. Every bit of training was tailored to that mission, that threat and that region.

Two weeks before we sailed, I remember sitting down on the mess deck about to start the working day when the CO made a pipe. You know that moment, when the whole mess goes quiet and everyone's waiting for what's coming? That was it. Then he said it: 'Change of tasking. You're going to the Falkland Islands. Eight months. Prepare accordingly.'

Brilliant.

The reaction was instant – a mix of lads booing, laughing, groans and swearing. Matelots at their best. Half of them reacted with, 'Typical.' The other half just stared at their mugs of tea, doing the mental maths of how they were going to tell their partners that Dubai flights were off and Christmas was no longer happening. In the RN we call this 'life in a blue one', meaning things can change on a sixpence, and you either crack on or get left behind.

Just like that, everything shifted: different mission, different risks, different climate. We had to retrain, reorganise, re-brief and reframe the entire deployment for the ship's company and we had to do it without losing momentum or morale. But it's hard to maintain morale thinking, 'Well, I won't need my beach shorts, but I'd best pack my thermal pants.'

For me, the next 24 hours were chaos on paper but controlled in practice. I had to sort kit changes, reorganise engineering priorities, steady the lads who were struggling and manage the dip in morale. Most disruption came from personal admin, lads realising birthdays, school plays, anniversaries and holidays were going to be missed. People will tolerate huge professional change but hit their home life and the frustration hits differently.

A young AB on my section pulled me aside, trying to act fine but clearly worried. His girlfriend was expecting their first baby, and he'd been told he'd be able to fly home for the birth. Now that we were being redirected to the other side of the world, anxiety was kicking in for him. Where would we be when she went into labour? Would he get back in time? No one knew, not the chain of command, not me, not him.

I couldn't fix it, but I could listen, level with him and help him get his head straight. Sometimes leadership isn't solving the problem; it's standing next to someone while they absorb it.

That's adaptability in action. It meant:

- changing plans without losing the team's trust
- adjusting communication styles across departments and ranks
- reassessing risks in real time
- making fast decisions with incomplete or conflicting information.

But most importantly, it meant keeping people calm and focused when the goalposts moved overnight – straight talking, a bit of banter. And letting lads drip (Navy slang for moan) – because Jack loves to drip – worked wonders. Once people got things off their chest, the mess settled. Sometimes venting is the pressure release valve that keeps the whole machine running.

As leaders, we don't just answer to the chain of command. Sometimes we're answering to the people who matter even more, like the child who thinks you'll be home for Christmas or the partner who's just been told that plans have changed again. That emotional weight adds pressure. And still, you've got to stay steady, lead the change and keep everyone else on track.

That experience and many more like it in the Navy taught me that adaptability means leading your team through change, even when you do not like it, while being steady, honest and with enough calm that they can borrow it from you.

And this isn't just a military thing either. Look at an NHS triage team during a winter surge. One minute they're dealing with a broken wrist, the next it's a cardiac arrest, then it's five patients from a motorway pile-up. The pace, the unpredictability, the stress, it's all real. But the team doesn't fall apart and they don't walk off the job because their shift ended. They keep going because someone steps up and leads through it with calm, clarity and control.

Flexibility isn't softness. It's resilience under pressure. Plans changing overnight is normal, not a failure. What matters is how you lead people through the shift.

8.3: Leadership in different contexts

What makes a great leader at sea makes a great leader ashore, if you know how to translate it. The conditions might change, but the core principles don't. Adaptability, clarity and calm under pressure are as valuable in a boardroom as they are in a machinery space.

In civilian life, adaptability shows up in all sorts of ways:

- a school head rewriting lesson plans after a sudden policy shift
- a retail manager adjusting to supply chain chaos without losing staff morale
- a public sector lead navigating yet another round of budget cuts
- a start-up founder pivoting the business after brutal customer feedback.

The biggest clash I noticed when working with civilian contractors wasn't skill, it was mindset. Matelots crack on, get the job done and keep standards high because that's how we're wired. Civilians, rightly, stick to rules, breaks and processes because their world is built differently. Neither side is wrong, but both can misunderstand each other badly if they don't adapt.

Risk appetite is worlds apart too. The Navy isn't reckless, not by a long shot, but we are used to solving problems fast and safely without ten layers of paperwork. Civilians often take a more cautious route – again, rightly so, but the pace mismatch can feel brutal when you're trying to hit a deadline.

And then there's the problem-solving mindset. In the Navy, if something needs doing, you muck in. In some civilian environments, you sometimes hear 'That's not my job', which can be a shock to someone used to everyone pitching in as a team. It doesn't make civilians lazy; it means the leadership culture values role boundaries differently. A good leader adapts to that rather than fights it.

One moment that always stuck with me came when I heard two contractors on a Friday afternoon openly saying they could 'drag this job out till tomorrow' because it was time and a half on Saturdays. That was a perfect example of how priorities differ. They were thinking about overtime; we were thinking about getting the job squared away so we could actually see our families: same task, completely different incentives.

On the flip side, I've seen what happens when a senior naval officer fires off emails to civilians using the same tone they'd use with sailors. In the Navy, that blunt, no-nonsense style is normal – it's efficient, expected and no one takes it personally. But drop that same tone into a civilian inbox and it can go down like a lead balloon.

When I worked as an instructor, I watched civilians open those emails and say, 'Who does this cheeky git think he's talking to? I'm not in the bloody Navy.' And to be fair, they had a point. Civvies haven't been conditioned to respond to rank, urgency or the 'do it now' culture we live by at sea.

The officer isn't being rude. Well, some are – they're communicating in the language they're used to. But outside the service, that same language can come across as demanding or even disrespectful. You have to read the room, know your audience and adjust your tone to suit.

People resist change; leaders help them through it. Adaptability applies everywhere, not just at sea.

8.4: Leading in dynamic environments

Adaptive leaders aren't made in classrooms; they're created in chaos. In the Navy, every day can throw something new at you: a machinery breakdown, a change in threat level mid-watch or a drill that suddenly turns real. You learn to think dynamically, switching leadership styles on the fly, reprioritising in minutes and updating the plan the second the facts change.

One moment that showed me the power of adaptive leadership had nothing to do with machinery or missiles. It happened on a beach in the Caribbean. The ship's company was having a barbecue and everyone was half-cut, sunburnt and joking about. A few of the crew thought they were in *Top Gun*, playing volleyball a few metres further down the beach. A lad went up to smash the ball over the net and landed like a sack of spuds, instantly yelling in pain. At first people laughed, thinking he was messing about. Then the realisation hit: he wasn't faking it. He'd done something serious to his arm. He'd gone over on his ankle, properly broken it and the shock was written all over his face.

What happened next was leadership in its purest form. The PO (Medical Assistant), essentially the ship's doc, went from relaxed and joking to laser focused in the space of a heartbeat. One minute she was chatting away with a beer in hand, the next she was kneeling beside him – calm, authoritative and completely in control. She reassured him, assessed the injury, got people moving and coordinated the whole response as if she'd been stone-cold sober for hours. The rest of us? Half-cut and confused, we were suddenly very glad she was there.

The atmosphere flipped instantly. What started as a laugh turned into concern and then into quiet, organised action. I remember feeling sorry for him, but mostly relieved that someone with her skill set was right there. Because the truth is, we'd have helped, of course we would, but it wouldn't have been the same quality of response – not even close.

What the team needed in that moment was everything at once: clarity, direction, reassurance and someone to stop the panic before it started. And she gave them exactly that. Her adaptability set the tone. As soon as she took charge, everyone else snapped into the role they needed to play. People who'd been drinking all afternoon suddenly became stretcher bearers and runners. The willingness of the crew to help was impressive, but it only worked because someone created order in the chaos.

Adaptive leadership means responding well when you do not know exactly what to do. It is the ability to shift styles instantly from relaxed to decisive, from social to structured, because the moment demands it. That's what keeps teams steady when the unexpected hits.

Civilian industries face the same volatility. In tech, finance, logistics and healthcare, the pace is relentless. Markets shift. Customers change. Systems fail. And only the leaders who stay mentally agile keep up.

Adaptability is the difference between chaos and control, no matter whether you're on a warship or a beach with a beer in hand.

8.5: Adaptability and change management

Change isn't a one-off; it's the job. And nowhere was that clearer than when I was an instructor at HMS *Sultan*, teaching students on the leading engineers course. On paper, they were all at the same career point. In reality, they were miles apart.

Some were razor-sharp but couldn't focus. Some were hands-on learners who needed everything shown, not spoken. Some had specific learning difficulties and needed more time. Others learned by repetition or by seeing it done right in front of them. Every trainee walked in with a different brain, a different level of confidence, a different pace. And if you try to teach one way to all of them, you instantly lose half the room.

I remember one lesson where a lad just couldn't grasp how a machine worked. I explained it cleanly, or so I thought, and the whole class nodded along, except him. His face dropped and suddenly the entire group was watching me to see what I'd do next. Moments like that can derail a whole session if you let them.

So I switched gears. I broke the operation down further – reframed it and related it to something he already understood. And then the penny dropped. You could see it in his face instantly. He even said, 'Ooo, I get it, that's simple. You should've said that at the start, chief.' Cheeky git. I genuinely enjoyed those moments because seeing understanding click into place never gets old.

It was clear that the lad felt under pressure to understand, the same as we all do when our peers get something we don't. And I felt under pressure to explain it in a way that landed for him. When people are under pressure, they don't need more information. They need the information they already have reframed so it makes sense. That is not a mentoring skill set; it's a leadership skill. And above all, it's adaptability.

What struck me wasn't that the trainee struggled, that's normal. It was how fast the atmosphere shifted. One person wobbles and suddenly the whole room feels it. But that is where adaptive leadership earns its keep. If you stay steady, the room steadies with you. If you adjust your approach, the group adjusts with you. You set the tone whether you realise it or not.

Once you accept that people learn and understand things differently, you stop teaching one way and start leading properly.

When change is led badly, whether in a classroom, an office or a corporate board, you get fear, resistance and confusion. But when it's led with clarity, patience and presence, people don't just cope with change, they move with it.

8.6: Adapt or be left behind

In a world of constant motion, your adaptability is the thing that keeps you relevant. Rigid leaders snap; flexible ones survive. And the teams who follow them survive, too.

If you can't adapt, you can't lead – not at sea, not in civvy street, not anywhere. The conditions will change. The plan will fall apart. People will wobble. And when that happens, everyone will look to you to set the tone.

You don't need to be the smartest person in the room. You don't need to have every answer. You just need to be the one who can pivot without losing your head, the one who keeps the team steady while everything else tilts.

I saw the downside of not adapting all the time.

In the dockyard, there were ex-matelots who had left the Navy years ago but still acted as if it was the early 1980s. 'We never did it like that before,' they would say. And I would think,

'Aye, because it is not 1984 anymore. Times have changed. Tech has moved on. Procedures have moved on. And we need to move with them.' Nostalgia is great, but stagnation kills productivity.

You see the same thing in civilian office environments. When I was working with civvies as an instructor, we had new teaching tech brought in, proper decent kit that would have made everyone's lives easier. But a handful of people just flat out refused to use it. They stuck to the old way: printing everything out, manual registers, clunky workarounds, the lot.

The moment that summed it up was when one of them said, 'I've always taught students this way.' And all I could think was, 'Yeah, and that's the problem.'

It's the same lesson as in the Navy. It doesn't matter if it's a ship or a classroom. If you refuse to adapt, the world moves on without you, and you just make life harder for yourself and everyone around you.

Ask yourself three things:

1. Do I shift gears when things go sideways?
2. Do I help my team adapt, or do I hold them in place?
3. Do I lead with calm and confidence when change rolls in?

If the answer is no, then here's the good news: adaptability can be learned. No one starts out great at it. You grow into it every time the plan collapses, every time you get blindsided and every time you choose to stay steady instead of spiralling.

And if the answer is yes? Then you're not just surviving change, you're driving it. That's what great leaders do.

So get a grip, learn to flex and crack on. The world isn't slowing down for you.

Chapter 9

Team building

No leader succeeds alone, no matter how good they think they are. The ability to build, shape and steer a team is what separates managers from leaders. And here's the truth: high-performing teams aren't built in theory; they're formed under pressure, trust and day-to-day graft.

In the Navy, you don't get to choose your crews. We got what we were given: a random mix of ages, personalities and backgrounds. But you learn quickly: when the job matters, difference doesn't divide, it strengthens. That only happens when leadership brings people together with purpose, clarity and shared standards.

This chapter is all about that: understanding team dynamics, building cohesion and aligning your crew, military or civilian, around what matters. You'll learn what makes teams tick, what breaks them apart and what your job is as the one in charge of keeping it all moving forward.

9.1: Diverse crews, unified teams

Leadership doesn't always begin when you feel ready. I found that out the hard way when I was given my local acting leading hand's rate on board a Type 42 destroyer. 'All well and good,' I thought. After all, I was already doing the job of a leading hand anyway. But then came the kicker: 'Oh, and you're also going to be killick of the mess.' The chief stoker laughed, enjoying the thought far more than I was.

In simple terms, that meant I was now responsible for an entire mess deck of around 40 hairy-arsed, testosterone-fuelled stokers, many of whom I'd shared beers, banter and rollockings with just days earlier. One minute, I was one of the lads; the next, I was the one responsible for 40 blokes who'd happily remind me of every mistake I made. Worse than that, I was now accountable for all of them, their actions, their standards and how that mess deck ran.

The mess itself was a proper melting pot. We had fresh-faced JRs straight out of training, still wide eyed and finding their feet. Then there were the seasoned leading hands, some of whom had clocked more time at sea than a Dover sole. Many of those blokes had mentored me the year before. They'd shown me the ropes when I was the new lad in the corner bunk. Now, suddenly, I was leading them.

It was awkward. No two ways about it.

Some of them backed me straight away. They knew what I brought to the table and were glad to see me stepping up. But others? Not so much. A few clearly thought they should've been given the role instead. A couple just ignored me entirely for the first few weeks, waiting to see if I'd sink or swim.

I didn't doubt my technical ability. I was a good engineer, I knew the kit and I could do the job. That wasn't the problem. The problem was leading people who'd seen and done more than I had. This wasn't just about turning spanners. This was about leading people who knew more than I did, had louder voices, bigger egos and in some cases, more credibility in the mess. I couldn't just act as if I was suddenly the boss and expect instant respect. But I couldn't be 'one of the lads' any more either. That was the tightrope and there's no handbook for walking it.

So, I leaned into emotional intelligence long before I even knew the term existed. I listened more than I talked. I stayed consistent, fair, decisive when I had to be and humble enough to admit when I didn't have the answer. When something needed doing, I mucked in. I didn't bark orders from the sidelines; I got my hands dirty.

Over time, the tension eased – not all at once, but slowly, one small leadership win at a time. Not because I nailed it overnight, but because I kept showing up the same way every day: steady, approachable, willing to graft and willing to lead. Eventually, we gelled into a strong, balanced team, one built on mutual respect, not just rank.

Looking back, I was ready for the promotion in terms of my technical ability. But I had no idea how much of a leap it would be in terms of responsibility. Managing a system is one thing. Managing a team and being accountable for every late return, every bit of kit left out, every attitude shift in the mess? That forced me to grow up fast.

In civilian teams the ingredients look different, but the pressure is the same: people watching to see if you're worth following. You might be leading people older than you, managing experts in areas you've never worked or trying to unify staff from departments, regions or backgrounds that don't normally mix. But the principle stays the same: leadership takes difference and turns it into strength.

9.2: Managing diverse teams

Civilian teams can be far more diverse than in the Armed Forces and I don't just mean ethnicity or gender. I'm talking about age, beliefs, communication styles, neurodivergence, family set-ups, ambition levels, priorities, politics, you name it.

In the Navy, we all wear the same uniform. On paper, that makes us look the same. But the truth is, personality was everywhere. You have the loud ones, the grafters, the clever quiet types, the jack-the-lads, the overthinkers and the odd one you were never quite sure about. It doesn't matter where someone is from, as long as they crack on when it counts. Good leadership recognises those differences and builds cohesion around them.

That means clear communication across roles, mutual respect, and instilling culturally aware leadership, even if we don't call it that. It also meant learning quickly how people think and react, because no two people do it the same way.

But in civvy street? Those differences are often front and centre. People *expect* to bring their whole selves to work. They don't just tolerate difference; they expect leaders to respect it. If you're used to a world of hierarchy, rules and thick-skinned banter, this shift can feel like a minefield at first. What worked on ship might not land in an open-plan office.

Knowing your audience applies to leadership as much as it does to storytelling.

Let me give you an example.

A few years back, I was working with a large engineering company (which shall remain nameless) in the dockyard. The ship's maintenance team was made up of a mix of matelots and civvy contractors. The civvies were all blokes, mostly in their late forties, who'd been with the company for years – good at their jobs, no doubt about it, but stuck in their ways.

The company had just brought in a young female engineer – bright, qualified, motivated and clearly eager to learn.

Problem was that the team weren't having it.

They didn't bully her outright, but they excluded her from the banter, palmed off the crap jobs without explanation and second-guessed her on everything. One day I overheard a contractor say to another, 'Just be careful what you say around her. She'll have you done for sexist jokes or summat.'

That line stuck with me. Why say that in this day and age? Why treat her like a threat, rather than part of the team?

And she noticed. Of course she did. And worse, she started to doubt herself. Her confidence took a hit. She spoke up less, withdrew in meetings and eventually asked to transfer departments – not because she wasn't capable, but because the environment made her feel as if she didn't belong.

This wasn't a competence issue; it was a culture issue.

The team didn't see the damage they were doing. But as a leader, you *must*. You set the tone. If people are being sidelined, excluded or made to feel like an outsider because they don't fit the mould, it's your job to step in, not because HR says so, but because it's the right thing to do. And because if you don't, you'll lose good people, quietly and quickly.

Leading diverse teams in civilian life means adjusting your approach without lowering your standards. You're not playing favourites. You're removing barriers so everyone can perform. That might mean:

- ⚓ being clear about what 'good' looks like
- ⚓ understanding how different people receive feedback
- ⚓ making space for quieter voices

- watching how your team interacts when you're not in the room
- and yes, reining in humour when it crosses the line.

The goal isn't to make everyone feel the same. The goal is to make everyone feel *included* and able to contribute without second-guessing whether they belong.

Diversity isn't a buzzword. It's your job. And if you get it right, your team will run through walls for you. As a leader, your team's success depends on your ability to bring out the best in people who think it through, say it straight, back it up with action and work differently from how you do. The good news is: if you've led a diverse mess deck under pressure, you're already halfway there. Now it's just about translating those instincts into a civilian context, with a bit more self-awareness and a bit less shouting.

9.3: Understanding team dynamics

A high-performing team doesn't form on paper; it's created through shared experience.

In the Navy, that meant:

- tough exercises
- long, boring watches
- laughter in the mess
- shared wins... and brutal losses.

It's those moments that built trust. Everyone knew who could be relied on at 03:00, who needed a push and who just needed a hand. That kind of awareness doesn't come from job titles – it comes from watching, listening and *leading*.

Civilian teams benefit from the same leadership mindset. They don't need forced fun days or monthly icebreakers; that's just going to annoy people. They need a leader who *gets it* – one who's tuned into the room, knows their people's strengths and quirks and adjusts their style accordingly.

Your job as a leader is to:

- learn how your people tick
- see how they react under pressure
- balance individual needs with team priorities.

Get that right, and something brilliant happens: the team starts to run itself. Not because you've stopped leading, but because you've built an environment where people trust each other, back each other and know what needs doing without waiting to be told.

9.4: Aligning people and purpose

Strong teams don't run on orders; they run on *clarity*. There's nothing worse than being handed a job by a leader that's either: a) something you're not trained to do; or b) so beneath your ability you could do it half asleep. Either way, it's demoralising. You start asking yourself, 'Why me? What's the point?'

We touched on this earlier when exploring team dynamics, but it's worth digging deeper here.

As a leader, your team needs to always understand three things:

- **why** they're here
- **what** success looks like
- **where** they fit in.

If they don't? You'll start to see the warning signs: confusion, frustration, finger pointing and morale dips that have nothing to do with laziness or bad attitudes. It's not that people *won't* do the job; they just don't see how their part fits into the bigger picture.

I've always believed that if morale dips, check the mission brief, not the team chat.

What that means is: stop blaming each other and go back to basics. Has the *why* behind the task been explained? Have we made the end goal clear?

Nine times out of ten, when something goes wrong, it's not because someone didn't care, it's because they didn't understand what was being asked or why it mattered.

The fix is simple, but not always easy:

- Start with a clear plan.
- Match people to jobs based on strengths, not just rank, rota or convenience.
- If the wheels wobble, don't reach for a scapegoat: revisit the structure.

Great leaders understand this: structure creates freedom. It gives your team confidence and clarity. And when you align that structure with purpose, when people *get* the mission and believe in it, that's when you unlock focus, energy and ownership.

9.5: Adair's action-centred leadership model

This is a model I've used across ships, departments and now in business. It's simple, but powerful. Adair's framework (1973) helps you lead with balance across three vital zones:

- **Task**: What needs doing? Prioritise, plan and set standards.
- **Team**: What does the group need? Drive collaboration, build cohesion and protect morale.
- **Individual**: Who needs support or a stretch? Tailor your leadership to the person, not just the role.

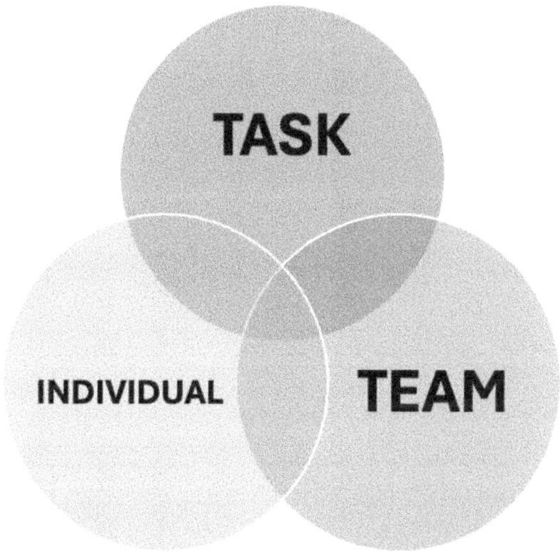

When one area gets too much focus, the others suffer and you won't spot it until cracks appear. Focus only on the task? Your people burn out. Focus only on people? The mission slips. Ignore the team dynamic? Silos form and trust breaks down.

Balance all three and your team thrives. Whether you're running a watch, managing a civilian team or heading up a project, this model will help keep your leadership grounded.

Chapter 10

Mentorship

If team building is about cohesion, mentorship is about growth. The best teams don't just perform; they develop. That means leaders aren't just delivering results – they're building people. Mentorship is how that happens, and it starts with you.

In any organisation, mentoring is part of the job. It's not optional. In the Navy, SRs are expected to shape JRs, not just in task, but in mindset, resilience and pride. That same mindset translates directly into civilian leadership. If you're not developing the people under your charge, you're not leading, you're just managing output.

This chapter explores the real-world power of mentoring: how to lead people as individuals, how to spot potential, how to guide without smothering and how to build future leaders who one day might replace you – and that's a win.

10.1: Learn, lead, repeat

Mentoring someone isn't a favour. It's a way of making your whole team stronger. In the Navy, mentoring is part of the culture, not a programme, not a side project. It's how leaders are made. Senior rates shape junior ones. Juniors learn, grow and pass it on. I can still name every mentor who shaped me, and I've seen the people I mentored go on to lead with strength, clarity and confidence. But here's the thing: mentoring goes both ways.

A young officer worth their salt will listen to everyone, from the SRs to the most junior ABs – not just to manage better, but to understand the world they're leading. You can't lead people unless you understand what they know, what they face and how they think. Sometimes, they'll know more than you do in certain areas. Good leaders don't see that as a threat; they see it as an asset. And that principle applies far beyond the military.

A few years back, the Navy was struggling to retain experienced engineers, especially at PO level. The solution? Bring in direct-entry POs from industry. It was a great plan in theory. These new senior recruits came in with serious technical ability but zero background in naval culture or leadership. One of them ended up in my mess deck.

Now, this guy was brilliant with systems. He knew the kit inside out – but leadership? Let's just say... not his strong point. He tried to manage everything himself, replying to every email, triple-checking work that didn't need it, hovering like a lost ghost in the engine spaces. I once found him polishing a control panel after the JR already had, because he didn't trust it had been done 'right'.

Meanwhile, the other POs were starting to murmur: 'He's a good bloke, but what's he doing on our pay scale? How'd he get his rate without earning his stripes?'

And that's the real danger. When someone's thrown into a leadership role they haven't been prepped for, it doesn't just rattle them – it rattles the team. It creates doubt and resentment and undermines cohesion before they even get a chance to settle. It wasn't his fault. The system set him up without the tools.

So, I took him aside and offered to help. We worked through a few basics: how to delegate clearly, how to back his team even when they did things differently, how to focus on leadership, not just control. He put the work in. The lads started warming to him. He found his groove. And the best part? Six months later, he started mentoring a new junior team lead himself.

That's mentorship – no titles, no training package, just experience, time and trust. Mentorship builds loyalty, confidence and leadership depth. But it only works if you treat it like part of your job, not something you'll 'get to eventually'. If you want better leaders in your organisation tomorrow, start mentoring them today.

10.2: Mentor like it matters

The best mentors don't just build competence – they build confidence. They don't just pass on skills – they shape belief.

When someone's under your wing, whether formally or just through shared time, your words carry weight. You might be the first person who's ever told them 'You've got leadership potential' or 'I see something in you'. That sticks. And it stays with them long after the task, the job or even the workplace has changed.

Mentorship does not have to involve lectures or life coaching. It's about showing up, paying attention and helping someone become the best version of themselves, not a copy of you.

Great mentors do four things well:

- ⚓ **Inspire** – through real stories, scars and vulnerability. You don't pretend you've always had it together. You show how you learned the hard way.
- ⚓ **Motivate** – not with slogans, but by noticing real progress and naming potential. 'That thing you did. That showed leadership.'
- ⚓ **Adapt** – to the person in front of you. Everyone learns differently. Good mentors flex.
- ⚓ **Challenge** – just enough to stretch someone without snapping them. You push, but you also catch them if they fall.

Mentorship means staying patient when they're struggling; letting them take a shot, even if they miss; telling them the truth when they're drifting, not to embarrass them, but to help them grow. And most of all, it means leading without the need for credit. Because when they succeed, that's your win too.

If you want better outcomes, you manage tasks. If you want better people, you mentor them. So mentor like it matters. Because it does.

10.3: What mentoring looks like in practice

Mentorship is built in the moments: how you show up, how you listen, how you guide without making it about you. It starts with intent.

If someone's under your wing, formally or not, you've got a chance to shape more than just their skills; you shape how they see themselves. That means recognising potential, offering challenge and showing that growth matters more than perfection.

And it's not one-size-fits-all. Great mentors tailor how they lead based on who's in front of them. Some people need a quiet nudge; others need a bold push. Some learn by watching, others by doing and some by talking it through. The best mentors flex without compromising standards.

Here's what that looks like in practice:

- **Observe, ask, listen:** Don't assume what someone needs. Watch how they work, ask what they want to improve, and listen without rushing in to fix.
- **Set boundaries:** You're not their best mate. Mentorship is built on trust, not overfamiliarity. Be supportive but stay professional and goal focused.
- **Teach inclusively:**
  - Show, don't just tell, for visual or hands-on learners.
  - Have conversations with those who process verbally.
  - Let people fail safely. Growth comes from trying.
- **Feedback is fuel**: Give honest, timely and useful feedback, not just noise. Praise effort, correct with care and always explain the why.
- **Make space for ownership:** Let them take the lead on something, even if they stumble. That stumble may teach more than a polished success.

Not everyone learns the same way. A good mentor adjusts their approach based on how the person in front of them takes in and processes information. The goal isn't to change your content, it's to change how you deliver it.

Learning style	What works best	Why it helps
Visual learner	Use diagrams, checklists, flowcharts, or live demos.	They absorb information through images and spatial awareness.
Verbal learner	Encourage them to talk through tasks or ideas.	Talking helps them clarify understanding and retain concepts.
Kinaesthetic learner	Let them try the task hands on, early and often.	They learn by doing; muscle memory reinforces learning.

Tip: mix your methods where you can. Even confident learners benefit from more than one mode of input.

Mentorship works when it's patient, personal and built on trust. You don't need all the answers; you need to be present, consistent and honest.

10.4: Futureproofing through mentorship

You won't be in charge forever – and that's the point. Good leadership means building people who can carry the torch, maybe even better than you could.

That requires trust. It means letting go of control and backing others to take the lead. It means creating a space where growth is normal, not occasional, where asking questions, making mistakes and learning out loud are encouraged.

If you're building a culture of mentorship, ask yourself:

- Have I made time for development, not just delivery?
- Do I challenge my team in ways that stretch them?
- Have I said out loud, 'You've got leadership potential'?

Those things matter more than we often realise. Many of us never hear it until someone makes a point of saying it. Be that someone. Mentorship is not only a responsibility; it's your legacy. You're not just building a better team. You're building future leaders. And if you do it right, they'll go further than you did. And that? That's a win.

Chapter 11

Communication

You can have the best plan, the best team and the best intentions. However, if you can't communicate clearly, confidently and consistently, you'll still fail. Great communication builds trust. It connects the why to the work. And under pressure, it keeps your team moving forward when they might otherwise freeze, flounder or fold.

Let me give you an example. I was working with a large MOD contractor firm, refitting and upgrading ships. It was a massive job with big moving parts and needed serious coordination. But every day started the same way: three-hour meetings repeating the same points, circling the same updates. Everyone tried to look as if they were contributing but no one was doing any actual work. That's not leadership. That's noise.

You could see the morale drain out of the room (especially among the matelots). People tuned out. No one knew what was expected because everything had been talked to death. It didn't matter how skilled or experienced anyone was; without clear communication, the whole thing dragged.

That's the thing about leadership: rambling doesn't cut it. Good communication means connecting, leading and getting the job done.

11.1: How are you perceived?

Ask yourself: 'How do I come across to others as a leader?' Your tone, body language and delivery style all send a message, whether you intend to or not. These things reveal your mindset, your confidence and, most of all, your approachability.

Let's take an example. An inexperienced lieutenant is tasked with giving an urgent order at sea. He avoids eye contact, then barks: 'You lot! Get over there and sort that shit out, now!' Then buries his head back in his clipboard.

His tone is short, his message vague ('What shit? Where?') and his posture closed. The effect? Confusion, resentment and a team that now feels talked *down* to, not led.

Now compare that to a seasoned PO watching it unfold. She calmly steps forward: 'Everyone, listen up – this is important. Here's what we need to do: all the equipment in that compartment needs to be secured and stowed properly. The sea state is about to get rough, and the last thing we want is gear flying around and someone getting hurt. Let's get this done quickly, and then we can go to lunch. If anyone isn't sure what needs to be lashed down, ask.'

Same team, same task. But her tone is calm. Her message is specific. She invites questions and speaks *with* the team, not *at* them. They don't follow her because of her rank; they follow because she communicates with clarity and respect. She doesn't shout. She leads. Your communication style *is* your leadership style. And your team will feel it, long before they follow your orders.

If you want a masterclass in clear communication, watch the RN's elite fighting force, the Royal Marines, deliver orders in the field – no fluff, no jargon, no 15-slide PowerPoint.

They keep it simple:

- Here's the situation.
- Here's the intent.
- Here's your role.
- Here's what success looks like.

It's direct, it's calm and it cuts straight to what people need to know right now. When rounds might start flying, there's no room for long-winded management waffle. And that approach works just as well in a boardroom as it does in a muddy field. People don't need speeches; they need clarity.

11.2: Tone and delivery

This is a big thing in civilian life. I've sat in project meetings where ten people around the table are all pulling in different directions, with questions, worries or points to make about their own bit of the job. The whole thing turns into noise. Then the project manager steps up. She raises a hand, brings the room back and cuts through the chaos: 'Right. Here's the situation. Here's what matters. Here's what each team needs to do next.'

The room settles instantly. People stop talking over each other. Everyone knows where they stand. That's communication. Not sounding clever, but bringing clarity when everyone else is getting lost in the detail.

Let's face it, not everyone sounds the same. In the RN, you'll meet people from all walks of life, including many who speak English as a second language. And in civilian teams? That diversity often goes even further. That's why your *tone* and *delivery* matter just as much as your words.

What you might be signalling:

Signal	Often perceived as
Calm tone, open posture	Confidence, approachability
Fast, clipped tone	Aggression, impatience
Monotone delivery	Boredom, detachment
Strong dialect and jargon	Confusion, inaccessibility
Slouched or fidgety posture	Lack of control or interest
Steady tone and eye contact	Engagement, credibility

We've moved past the days of clipped, upper-class officer accents, but the truth is, people still make snap judgements based on how someone speaks. Accents, dialects and pace can all shape how you're perceived as a leader, sometimes unfairly, but still very much in play. That doesn't mean you need to change who you are. But it does mean you should *adapt* how you speak, depending on your team.

If you've got a strong regional accent or use heavy slang, slow down. Trim the jargon. Speak clearly. It's not dumbing down; it's about opening up. A few examples:

- A sharp, fast-paced delivery can come across as aggressive or impatient.
- A monotone voice may suggest boredom or disinterest.
- A friendly, measured tone? That builds approachability and trust.

And your body language backs it all up. Are you making eye contact? Slouching? Crossing your arms? These non-verbal cues often say more than your words do.

This doesn't mean pretending to be someone else; it's about making sure your message *lands*.

If people aren't understanding you, ask yourself:

- Do I need to slow down?
- Could I simplify this?
- Am I backing up my words with body language?

Your message hasn't been delivered when *you've said it*, it's delivered when *they understand it*.

11.3: Body language

Your body speaks long before your voice does, and often with more honesty. How you stand, move and hold eye contact shapes whether others see you as confident, credible and approachable.

Ask yourself, am I:

- **Open and inviting**: Steady eye contact, a calm posture and the occasional nod show you're present and engaged. It signals that you're listening, not just waiting to talk.
- **Closed or defensive:** Crossed arms, shifting your gaze or fidgeting can give the impression of discomfort or disinterest, even when you mean well.
- **Dominant or overbearing:** Standing too close, looming over someone, or using exaggerated gestures can feel aggressive or intimidating. Keep your movements deliberate and your presence respectful.

Whatever the situation, your demeanour should match the moment. Composure and focus convey professionalism. In contrast, slouching or appearing distracted suggests you're unprepared or disconnected.

Remember, your accent or dialect can add authenticity, but clarity should always be your priority. If you're unsure whether you're coming across in the way you intend, slow down, ask for feedback or watch yourself on video – it's one of the fastest ways to spot unhelpful habits.

Quick reference: what you may be signalling:

Body language	Often perceived as
Open posture, steady eye contact	Confidence, openness
Crossed arms, little eye contact	Defensiveness, detachment
Looming or over-gesturing	Aggression, dominance
Slouched or distracted	Lack of focus, low energy

Your body is part of your message. Make sure it's reinforcing, not undermining, your words.

11.4: Swearing, style and professionalism

Professional communication comes down to being clear, respectful and credible, not sounding fancy. Whether you're delivering bad news, giving instructions or just chatting over a brew, how you carry yourself sets the tone for everyone around you.

Small mannerisms make a big difference. Sighing, rolling your eyes or glancing at your phone mid-conversation will undermine your message, no matter how polite your words are. The same goes for sloppy language or constant swearing. A well-placed expletive can show authenticity and passion, but if every other sentence is a swear word, it quickly signals disrespect or a lack of self-control.

Professionalism also means adapting your communication style to fit the situation:

- **Formal settings**: be structured, precise and composed.
- **Informal settings**: be relaxed and conversational but stay respectful.
- **Stressful situations:** stay calm, avoid sarcasm and focus on solutions.

While working out of an overseas base port (which again shall remain nameless), we had a civilian contractor assigned to support and maintain some rather specialist kit fitted on board the ship. He had all the technical skill you could ask for, but no filter whatsoever. He'd turn up late, swear in every sentence and crack jokes about everyone from the senior officers to the ABs.

At first, people tolerated it, either because he knew his job or possibly because of his intimidating presence and larger-than-life personality. But over time, the novelty wore thin. His credibility evaporated, and when something genuinely important came up, no one took him seriously. It wasn't his knowledge that held him back; it was how he carried himself.

That's the reality: you can be brilliant on paper, but if your mannerisms and attitude undermine respect, your leadership will never stick.

Here's a quick reference to keep in mind whenever you're communicating as a leader:

Action	Why it matters
Listen fully before responding.	Shows respect, builds trust and avoids misunderstandings.
Watch your non-verbal cues.	Your body language often speaks louder than your words.
Keep language clear and controlled.	Prevents confusion and maintains credibility.
Show up prepared, even under pressure.	Demonstrates reliability and reinforces confidence.
Be the calmest person in the room.	Sets the tone for composure and professionalism.

11.5: The three Cs of communication

Keep this in your pocket for every conversation, presentation or tasking brief:

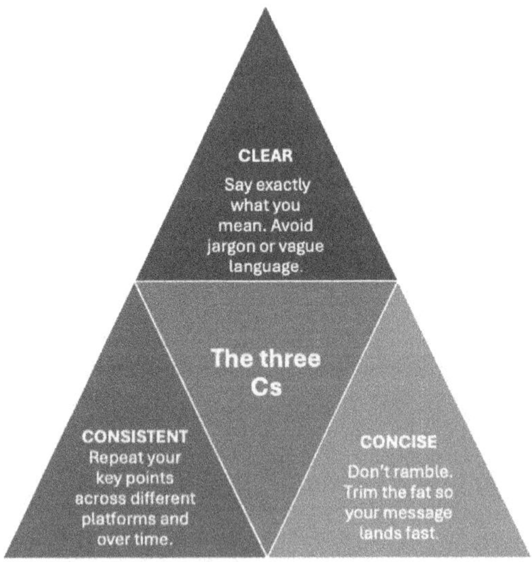

Whether you're briefing a team, writing an email or giving feedback, the three Cs will help you communicate with impact. These principles reflect communication practices consistently reinforced within RN leadership and training environments and embedded in formal defence writing and command doctrine.

11.6: Tactical comms tip

Clear communication is one of the most practical ways to build trust and credibility as a leader. When your message lands well, teams act faster, mistakes shrink and morale stays high.

Here are four tactics that turn good communicators into great ones:

Tactical communications tips	
Active listening	Don't just wait for your turn to speak. Show that you're listening. Ask clarifying questions and summarise what you've heard.
Message tailoring	Speak differently to a junior sailor than you would to the CO. The same applies to a senior executive versus a new apprentice. Adjust your tone, format and pace to suit your audience.
Feedback loops	Always check for understanding. Asking 'Does that make sense?' doesn't show weakness – it shows you care.
Story-telling	If you want your message to stick, use a story. Just one. Keep it short and anchor the point in something human.

Master these four skills and you'll communicate with clarity, credibility and impact, no matter who's in the room.

11.7: Structure is power

This is something I have a personal gripe with. I hate sitting in meetings around a table just talking about things that could easily be shared in an email or going over the same points again and again. I hate it when people feel they have to put in their two cents just to be seen. Let's just get on with the job rather than talk it to death.

As I mentioned at the start of this chapter, I worked with a large MOD contractor firm tasked with refitting and upgrading ships. It was a massive project that required complex management. But when you spend three hours a day talking about progress and what's next, that's three hours you're not actually doing the work. It's unproductive and unmotivating.

Rambling doesn't build clarity. It just makes people switch off. You can almost see the interest drain from the room when a meeting drags on with no purpose or clear outcome.

The answer is simple: get to the point. A few small changes can transform communication:

- daily 15-minute stand-ups
- a shared digital task board
- a clear comms chain.

Delays will be cut in half. Morale goes up. People still feel informed and trusted and they can get on with the work.

Great communicators don't just talk. They connect. They listen. They adapt.

When the pressure's on, structure helps you stay clear and credible. Instead of assuming you've been understood, take time to confirm it. Instead of broadcasting the same way to everyone, tailor your message to your audience and the moment.

If you're doing that consistently, you're not just speaking, you're leading.

Chapter 12

Unconscious bias

Unconscious bias is what happens when our brains take mental shortcuts and form fast, automatic assumptions about people based on surface details: their appearance, accent, age, gender, background or how much they remind us of ourselves. It's not always intentional. It doesn't mean we're bad people – it just means we're human. Psychologists such as Daniel Kahneman call these shortcuts 'heuristics' – quick-fire mental rules we use to make decisions without thinking. They're useful, but they often lead us in the wrong direction.

Picture a pod of dolphins swimming together, flipping and squeaking in sync. Along comes an octopus – different shape, different sounds, different way of moving. The dolphins pause, look at each other and think: 'Who's this guy? He's not one of us.'

It may be a daft example, but it proves the point: we instinctively trust what feels familiar. And that's where bias begins.

I've seen unconscious bias play out on ships in subtle ways. A new joiner arrives from training to their first ship with a strong regional accent and a quieter, more measured way of speaking. No one says anything outright, but they're questioned more closely, their answers are double-checked and they're slower to be trusted.

Nothing they've done warrants that treatment. They've met every standard required to be there and passed the same training as everyone else. The hesitation comes from unfamiliarity, not competence or commitment. The bias isn't deliberate, but it's there all the same.

The opposite bias shows up too. People who sound more polished or 'posh' are often assumed to be more capable or intelligent, even when there's no evidence to support it.

12.1: Why bias matters in leadership

As humans, we don't make decisions based purely on logic. Research consistently shows that most of our judgements happen before we're even aware we've made them (Bargh & Chartrand 1999; Kahneman 2011). Our subconscious plays a significant role in shaping our thoughts, behaviours and the way we interact with others. This is especially true in leadership, where unconscious bias can influence how we perceive people, how we assign tasks and how we build the team dynamic needed to succeed.

In the Navy, trust, teamwork and clear communication are critical. Yet even in such disciplined environments, our biases can affect who we listen to, who we rely on and who we choose to develop or promote. For example, it's easy to assume that a confident, outspoken team member is more capable than their quieter but equally skilled shipmate.

We often mistake confidence for competence, give more weight to those who speak up and assume that personality automatically signals ability. Research in organisational psychology and leadership consistently shows that these snap impressions are unreliable (Tversky & Kahneman 1982). Quieter individuals may be just as capable and sometimes more so, but get overlooked because their competence is less visible.

12.2: Diversity and inclusion

You might hear 'unconscious bias' and think, 'Ah, that's all D&I stuff.' Well, yes and no.

Yes – recognising unconscious bias is crucial to preventing exclusion and driving meaningful change where it's needed. It's the mechanism behind why diverse teams consistently outperform homogeneous ones, a pattern that has been demonstrated across business, public sector and organisational research for decades (McKinsey & Company 2020; Page 2007).

However, true leadership requires more than simply following policies and procedures to tick the compliance box. To lead effectively, you must engage with people on a personal level.

Beyond any legal requirements, embracing diversity means creating an inclusive environment where every team member feels valued, respected and able to contribute, regardless of their differences. It's about recognising the unique perspectives and strengths that a diverse team brings.

Understanding and addressing bias, both personally and within your team, means questioning your own assumptions. Are your perceptions based on facts, or are they shaped by personal experiences, cultural norms and social stereotypes? Our biases can be influenced by upbringing, media narratives and the environments we've worked in. Psychological research shows that these influences often become our 'default settings' unless we consciously challenge them (Bargh & Chartrand 1999; Greenwald & Banaji 1995).

By taking the time to reflect on these influences, you can start to challenge ingrained thoughts and make more informed, fair decisions as a leader. When you do, you create a culture that doesn't just tolerate diversity but values it, and that's when real progress happens.

12.3: Types of unconscious bias

Research into how people think and make decisions shows that we all carry a set of built-in biases (Tversky & Kahneman 1982; Kahneman 2011). These biases operate automatically, often without us realising it, and they influence who we trust, who we listen to and how we judge competence and potential in others.

As I've established, if you want to be a fair and effective leader, you must first recognise the different types of bias so you can make more objective decisions. Some of the most common biases in the workplace include:

Unconscious bias	
Affinity bias	This occurs when we prefer people who are like us. For example, a leader may unconsciously form a stronger connection with a team member simply because they share a home town or support the same football team. Over time, this can lead to favouritism and unequal opportunities.
Confirm-ation bias	This happens when we seek out information that confirms our pre-existing beliefs while ignoring evidence that contradicts them. For instance, if a leader assumes a new team member isn't competent, they might only notice that person's mistakes and overlook their successes.
Halo effect	The tendency to let one positive trait overshadow all other qualities. For example, assuming that a highly charismatic employee is also an excellent leader, even if they lack the necessary experience or skills.
Horns effect	The opposite of the halo effect: one negative trait influences our overall perception of a person. For example, if an employee struggles with public speaking, their manager might wrongly assume they are also poor at written communication or problem solving.
Gender bias	This occurs when assumptions are made about someone's abilities or leadership potential based on gender. For example, a female officer may be overlooked for a physically demanding role, despite meeting all requirements, simply because of outdated stereotypes about strength and endurance.
Racial bias	When judgements about a person's skills, intelligence or work ethic are influenced by race rather than actual performance. For example, an employee from an ethnic minority group may have to work harder to prove their capabilities compared to their peers, due to unconscious biases in the workplace.
Age bias	Making assumptions about a person's abilities based on their age rather than their individual skills. For example, assuming an older employee is resistant to change or struggles with technology, or assuming a younger employee lacks leadership skills due to inexperience.

Recognising these common biases is the first step towards more fair, inclusive leadership. By understanding how bias can influence your decisions, you put yourself in a stronger position to challenge assumptions, build trust and create an environment where every team member has the opportunity to thrive.

12.4: How leaders can overcome unconscious bias

Our brains process vast amounts of information every second, often relying on mental shortcuts (the aforementioned heuristics). These shortcuts help us make quick decisions with minimal effort. Kahneman describes this as 'thinking fast' – instinctive and automatic. It's useful, but prone to error. Think of it like your phone's autocorrect: it speeds things up but often changes the message entirely. Unconscious bias works the same way – it shapes our judgements in ways we don't always realise.

As a leader, recognising and addressing these biases is key to building a fair and inclusive workplace. It's not about meeting diversity quotas – it's about creating an environment where all team members' skills and contributions are valued.

Here are some ways in which you can reduce unconscious bias in your leadership:

- **Self-reflection:** regularly challenge your own assumptions and be aware of your personal biases.
- **Seek diverse perspectives:** encourage input from different team members to avoid groupthink and broaden your understanding.
- **Use objective criteria:** base decisions on skills, performance and facts rather than gut feelings.
- **Promote inclusivity:** ensure every team member feels valued and has equal opportunities to contribute.

Remember, bias isn't a personal flaw; it's part of being human. The key is recognising it and actively working to overcome it. Avoid relying solely on 'gut instinct' decisions, which may be influenced by bias. Instead, ground your choices in clear evidence of someone's skills and performance to create fairer outcomes.

Surround yourself with people from diverse backgrounds and listen actively to what they have to say. Encouraging a range of perspectives helps reduce blind spots and improves decision making. Before making assumptions about your team members, ask yourself:

1. Would I think the same way if this person looked, sounded or behaved differently?
2. Am I giving everyone an equal opportunity to prove themselves?

By consistently reflecting on these questions, you set a higher standard for yourself and for those you lead.

12.5: Inclusion in action

Unconscious bias is like a hidden compass – it steers our judgements and influences who we listen to, trust or overlook. It's not malice, it's mental autopilot. But as a leader, your job is to fly manually. As mentioned before, diversity isn't about meeting quotas. Inclusion isn't a slogan. And bias isn't fixed by attending one training day. It's a discipline, practised daily in small choices.

Try these:

- Pause before deciding. Again ask yourself: 'Would I think the same if this person looked or sounded different?'
- Use structured criteria when hiring or assessing performance.
- Rotate who speaks first in meetings.
- Seek feedback from the margins, not just the centre.

True leadership means creating an environment where:

- different views are welcomed
- every voice feels safe to speak
- performance, not familiarity, drives opportunity.

Unchecked bias leads to exclusion. Inclusion, on the other hand, unlocks engagement, creativity and cohesion. When you lead with awareness, you set a higher standard, not just for yourself, but for everyone who follows.

Chapter 13

Integrity and ethics

Leadership involves making decisions, then living with them. Integrity and ethics don't usually show up when things are easy, when the rules are clear or when everyone agrees. They show up under pressure. When time is short. When the right answer costs more than the wrong one. When nobody's watching, or worse, when everyone is watching and expecting you to bend.

Integrity, in its simplest form, is alignment. It's doing what you say you'll do. It's holding the same standard when it's inconvenient as you do when it's comfortable. Not because there's a rulebook, but because you've decided where your line is and you refuse to step over it.

Ethics goes one step further. It comes down to the impact of your decisions on other people, not just your behaviour. Who carries the risk? Who pays the price? Who benefits? And who gets hurt when things go wrong? Ethics lives in the grey space between competing priorities, where every option has a cost and someone is going to be unhappy.

In the Royal Navy, this isn't theoretical. Decisions made in an engine room, on the bridge or in a control room have real consequences. Get it wrong and people can be injured, equipment can be lost or lives can be put at risk. That reality forces you to think beyond shortcuts, convenience or self-interest. You don't just answer for what you did – you answer for what happened.

Civilian leadership doesn't usually carry the same immediate physical danger, but the ethical weight is still there. Trust, safety, livelihoods, reputation and culture all sit on the back of everyday decisions. The difference is that in civilian life, the consequences are often delayed, diluted or quietly absorbed by someone else. That makes ethical drift easier and integrity harder to hold.

This chapter is about being consistent, not perfect. It's about understanding where your line is before pressure forces you to find it the hard way. Because when things get difficult, you won't rise to your values. You'll fall to whatever you've actually been practising.

And as a leader, whether you like it or not, people are watching where you land.

13.1: The weight of responsibility

On board a warship, responsibility isn't abstract. One engineering oversight can mean system failure, environmental damage or worse. You don't just carry out a task; you carry the outcome. That's what separates leadership from management.

Take environmental protection at sea. A single poor decision, a missed detail or an incorrect assumption can result in pollution that damages marine life, affects coastal communities and draws serious legal attention.

On paper, the rules are clear. In practice, this is where pressure creeps in.

Maybe the tank is fuller than expected. Maybe you're running late. Maybe there's pressure to keep systems online, meet the programme or deal with the next job waiting behind this one.

In moments like that, things get assumed rather than checked. Tasks get rushed, handovers aren't done and people rely on the system working the way it usually does. Not because anyone wants to cause harm. Not because people don't care about the environment. But because they're human.

When pollution happens, responsibility doesn't stop with the person who turned the valve. It travels upward. It lands on the department, the chain of command and the leader who signed it off, supervised the job or failed to ask the right questions.

Careers end over decisions like that. So does trust.

That's the weight of responsibility.

Real leaders don't hide behind procedures or rank. They don't pass the buck downward when things go wrong. They accept that if it happened on their watch, it's theirs to own. That doesn't mean blaming yourself for everything. It means being accountable for standards, oversight and decisions.

You might not be dealing with ships or environmental law, but the principle holds. If a safety rule is bypassed, a compliance check missed or an ethical line crossed without anyone noticing in time, the responsibility doesn't disappear just because you weren't the one who physically did it.

Owning that responsibility means stepping up early, correcting course and learning how to stop it happening again. That's what builds trust. That's what earns respect. And that's what tells your team exactly where the line is, without you ever having to shout about it.

13.2: Know what you stand for

When pressure hits, you don't suddenly become a better leader. You fall back on your habits and the standards you already live by.

Knowing what you stand for does not come from memorising values or quoting them in meetings. It comes from knowing where your line is before you are tired, rushed or under scrutiny. Because when those moments arrive, you will not have time to think it through properly. You will default to whatever feels normal.

In the Navy, the core values are drilled into you early: courage, commitment, discipline, integrity and respect. They're simple words, but they only mean anything when they cost you something. When courage means speaking up. When discipline means slowing things down. When integrity means saying no, even when yes would be easier and more convenient.

Imagine you're the shift supervisor in a busy warehouse. A pallet hasn't been secured properly. It's not dramatic. No one's hurt. But it's unstable. You're already behind schedule, the lorry's waiting and fixing it means delaying dispatch and answering awkward questions.

You've got a choice. You can walk past it and hope nothing happens. You can tell yourself it's not your job. Or you can stop the line, deal with it properly and accept the delay. That moment tells your team far more about what you stand for than any values poster ever could.

13.3: Set the standard

Culture: it's something you build day by day through what you let slide and what you stop. You're not trying to create a 'nice' culture. You're creating a culture where standards are clear, corners aren't cut and people know the line won't move just because things get busy or uncomfortable.

People watch leaders closely, especially under pressure. If cutting corners gets you through the day with less hassle, people will cut corners. If safety only matters after something's gone wrong, people will take chances until it does.

Go back to that warehouse pallet. Walk past it once and people notice. Walk past it again and it becomes normal. Before long, 'we'll sort it later' becomes the accepted way of working. That's how standards slip. Not because people are bad, but because small compromises go unchallenged over a period of time.

This is where ethics becomes real – not in policies or statements, but in everyday decisions. Who takes the risk? Who gets protected? And who ends up carrying the consequences when something fails?

I heard a saying a lot in the Navy: 'I don't make the rules, I just enforce them.' It always bugged me. Not because the rules were wrong, but because this was often used to dodge responsibility. You might not write policy, but you decide how it's applied – what you're strict about, what you overlook, who gets pulled up and who gets a quiet word. That's not neutral – that's leadership. And that's where culture actually lives.

As a leader, you're setting that tone whether you mean to or not. What you ignore sends just as strong a message as what you challenge. In the end, culture is simple. It's what your team believes is acceptable when you're not in the room.

13.4: The decisions people remember

Ethics show up when the answer isn't clean and the pressure is on. It's delaying a job because the safety check isn't right, knowing it'll annoy someone senior. It's calling out a person's behaviour because it crosses a line. It's backing a junior member of the team who followed the rules, even when it would be easier to sacrifice them to keep the peace.

These decisions rarely feel good in the moment. They cost time, convenience and, worst of all, a leader's popularity. But they're the decisions people remember. They're the moments when trust is either built or broken.

People won't remember every order you give or every success you deliver. They'll remember whether you stood your ground when it mattered and most of all when you stand up for your team.

Integrity is what keeps you steady when pressure is pulling you in different directions. Responsibility is the weight that comes with the role. Strong leaders don't avoid it – they carry it.

So ask yourself:

- What do I consistently allow when I'm under pressure?
- Where have I chosen convenience over standards?
- If my team copied my behaviour exactly, would I be comfortable with the result?

Ethics aren't about what you do when it's easy. They're about who you are when it costs you something. Leadership is being willing to pay that cost first.

Chapter 14

Learning and development

The best leaders I served with weren't the loudest, the flashiest or the ones with a chest full of medals. They were the ones who never thought they'd cracked it. Even after 20 years, they still asked questions, still listened, still learned. The ones who struggled? Nine times out of ten, it was the blokes who thought they knew it all. The sea has a fast way of proving otherwise. Learning isn't optional out there. Leadership means being the one who keeps improving, not the one who thinks they are already the smartest in the mess.

In the RN, learning isn't optional; it's the rhythm of daily life. And no, it's not just about drills or warfare. You train to think smarter, lead stronger and recover faster when things go sideways. From day one, you're taught that learning is part of the job. Rank isn't a status; it's a standard. And that standard must be upheld every single day through resilience, reflection and constant development.

That mindset transfers perfectly to civilian leadership. The world doesn't stand still. Teams evolve. Technology changes. Industries transform overnight. What worked last year might not even make sense tomorrow. The leaders who thrive are the ones who never stop asking: 'How can I do this better?'

14.1: Lifelong learning

Leadership development isn't a workshop or a performance review check box. It's a career-long, mindset-driven commitment. You can learn from mentors, training and books like this one, and you should. But real growth comes from experience, and more importantly, how you reflect on it.

Most of us ignore advice when we're young because of pride, inexperience or the belief that we know better. Sometimes we do. But more often, we take a few knocks, realise we've over-estimated ourselves and finally hear the wisdom we were too stubborn to listen to earlier.

Great leaders listen sooner. They learn faster. And they treat failure not as a reason to retreat, but as fuel to improve.

One of the biggest barriers to learning as a new leader isn't lack of training, it's fear: fear of looking inexperienced in front of your team; fear of looking weak in front of those above you. So instead of asking early, we bluff, we stall or we try to quietly fix things ourselves and hope no one notices.

I learned this the hard way as a young leading hand. We had a machinery issue just as we were about to sail. Nothing dramatic, but time critical. A bit of kit had tripped and I was sent to reset it on the control panel. 'No problem,' I said, full of confidence. I got to the panel, which to be fair wasn't marked up brilliantly, and had a complete brain fart. What do I press to reset it?

And that's where I made it worse. Instead of asking for help, I cracked on, convinced I *should* know what to do. After all, I was a leading hand. But the truth was, I'd forgotten, and my pride told me I could wing it. I didn't want to look stupid.

Long story short, I ended up turning to one of the young engineers next to me and saying, 'Oi, is it that one you press?'

'Yes mate,' he replied, with a grin I still remember.

That was it. And it stuck with me, because the mistake wasn't the issue. My reluctance to ask for help was. From that point on, I listened earlier, involved the right people sooner and improved faster because of it. That's what learning in leadership really looks like – not pretending you've got all the answers, but having the humility to get to the right answer quicker.

14.2: Lessons from failure (and success)

When things go wrong in the Navy, we don't sweep it under the carpet. We debrief – properly.

- What happened?
- Why did it happen?
- What will we do differently next time?

It can be uncomfortable. It demands honesty, tactical clarity and quick turnarounds. But that's how we improved. You learn. You adapt. And the next time, you're sharper.

That's what real development looks like:

- **Repetition**: Getting the reps in. Leadership is built through action.
- **Reflection**: Stepping back and asking, 'What worked? What didn't?'
- **Responsiveness**: Applying the lesson quickly and deliberately.

In civilian leadership, this matters just as much. Whether you're running a sales team, managing a hospital or leading a start-up, setbacks are inevitable. The best leaders don't take them personally, but they *do* take them seriously. They bounce forward, not just back.

And it's not just failure that teaches. If something worked, figure out why. What made the difference? Who stepped up? Where were the blockers cleared? Great leaders learn from the wins as well as the wounds.

14.3: Sharpen your edge

No one graduates from leadership. What worked with one team might flop with the next. The generation you're leading today doesn't think like the one from five years ago. Markets change. People change. *You* change.

Leadership demands constant recalibration.

And the good news? You don't have to get everything right on day one. But you do have to stay humble and keep showing up, ready to learn, adapt and get sharper.

14.4: Tools that help you grow

Growth doesn't happen by accident. It happens when you build the right habits and use the right tools:

- ⚓ **Self-reflection**: Own your blind spots. Ask yourself what could've gone better and what to do next time.
- ⚓ **Feedback**: It's not always comfortable, but it's almost always useful. Ask for it. Take it on the chin. Use it.
- ⚓ **Mentorship**: Find someone who's walked the road ahead. Learn from their missteps, not just their victories.

If you're the one doing the mentoring, not just receiving it, Chapter 10 has you covered with tips, tools and mindset shifts to help you build others up.

In the military, feedback is often blunt – and sometimes public. Why? Because lives are on the line. If someone's going to make a mistake that risks equipment, operations or lives, you don't sugar-coat it. You speak up, loud and clear. The stakes demand it.

In civilian settings, feedback tends to be softer, more measured, often delayed and easier to ignore. But that doesn't mean the consequences are always minor. Just because you're not on a warship doesn't mean lives aren't at risk.

I once watched a warehouse supervisor get a roasting – public, direct and deserved – from the dockyard safety officer. A forklift had clipped a racking leg that had already been flagged as unstable. Instead of cordoning off the area, the team leader ignored the report and carried on operations as normal. An hour later, half the shelf collapsed. No one was injured, but only by pure luck.

The manager tore into him. It wasn't diplomatic. It wasn't gentle. But it was fair. The key lesson? Whether it's given gently or wrapped in a full-blown rollocking, feedback is *still* feedback. If it's right, own it. Don't sulk. Don't justify. Learn from it. Take it on the chin, adjust and crack on.

Chapter 15

Morale, motivation and momentum

Morale doesn't collapse all at once. It drains slowly, like water through a cracked bulkhead. You don't always hear it happening. But if you're not paying attention, it'll be gone before you know it.

I was once on a deployment where we spent week after week at sea. Watches dragged on without proper downtime. Equipment kept breaking. The routine was relentless. Every day blurred into the next.

Yes, we all knew the deal. It's the job – long hours, cramped conditions, operational stress. No one joins the Navy expecting spa days. But here's the thing: even when you accept the pressure, you're still human. And without space to decompress, even the strongest crews start to fray.

One night I walked into the mess deck, expecting the usual piss-taking and banter over a brew. Instead, it was dead quiet – not out of focus, but burnout. Eyes were down, shoulders slumped. Lads who normally had plenty to say just sat there, drained.

That's when it hit me. The job wasn't just technical, it was emotional. And if I didn't start leading from that space, we weren't just going to lose performance. We were going to lose the team long before we lost the ship.

Motivation isn't about hype. It's not about rousing speeches or sticking up 'You've got this!' posters in the corridor. Real motivation is about helping people feel seen, heard and valued, even when they're knackered, frustrated or far from home.

It's about showing them that what they do matters. That they matter.

15.1: Motivation is personal

Everyone's got their own reason for turning up. For some, it's pride in the job. For others, it's the wage, career progression or simply not letting the team down. Some people are driven by recognition, while others just want to feel useful and respected.

Motivation is personal. What fires up one person might do nothing for the next. That's why blanket approaches rarely work and shouting louder almost never helps.

Your job as a leader goes beyond getting results. It is about understanding what drives your people to deliver them. And that means tuning into the emotional side of leadership, not just the task list.

This is where emotional intelligence kicks in (see also section 3.3). Not the fluffy corporate poster version, but the actual day-to-day skill of reading your team and adjusting how you lead.

EQ is about:

- knowing how you show up under pressure
- clocking the mood of your team before it unravels
- delivering feedback in a way that lands, not just unloads
- sensing when motivation's dipping, even if the work's still getting done.

In the Navy, it mattered. You could have someone nailing the drills, but if they were emotionally shot, it was only a matter of time before something cracked. EQ helped you spot that early, before it became a safety issue.

It looks like:

- noticing when a usually chatty worker goes quiet and checking in
- holding back when someone's on the ropes instead of barking orders

- reading the energy of the mess deck, shop floor or office and adjusting your tone
- learning what makes each person tick, not just what motivates you.

Good leaders don't just track output. They track people. Some still think this stuff is fluffy. It's not. It's professional awareness. You still hold people to standards, still demand results. But you do it smarter, by understanding the emotional engine under the surface.

Because leadership is about more than what gets you out of bed. It is about what keeps your team going when the pressure is on, morale is low and there is no end in sight.

15.2: The power of recognition

Never underestimate the impact of a well-timed 'thank you'. It doesn't have to be grand. Just real and right when it's needed most.

A few years back, during operational sea training (OST) out of Plymouth, we were having a rough time of it. Days were packed with high-intensity drills, firefighting, flooding, wartime damage control scenarios – and nights weren't much better. Instead of getting any downtime, we were stuck alongside, fixing a growing list of mechanical defects. Two weeks of that pace and we were exhausted.

Morale was dropping hard. And it wasn't us that flagged it; it was the MEO and the heads of department who noticed and felt it was only right the CO should be made aware. While other departments were heading ashore to grab a pint and let off steam, the engineers were still down in the guts of the ship, elbows deep in problems that couldn't wait.

That's when the CO stepped in. No speech, no ceremony – he just pulled the engineering teams together, wheeled a crate of beer into the workshop and said something simple like, 'I know you're grafting harder than anyone right now. This is just a small nod to say we see it.'

It wasn't about the beer. It was about the moment. Junior and senior engineers side by side, stripped of rank (just for a second), reminding them that someone above them was paying attention. That gesture lit a spark. We cracked on as a tighter unit, with a bit more fight in us, because we felt seen.

In the civilian world, this kind of recognition could look like:

- a public shout-out during a Monday team huddle
- a handwritten note left on someone's desk
- a one-liner in passing: 'You've been smashing it. I see it.'

It doesn't take a bonus scheme or a budget line – just emotional awareness, timing and the willingness to show your team that their effort isn't invisible.

15.3: When focus falters

When teams lose their edge, most leaders get louder. They bark orders, ramp up pressure and demand results. But shouting doesn't fix fatigue. It just drowns it out for a bit.

What works better is reflection. Not navel-gazing, not management speak, just honest assessment before you start throwing solutions at the wall.

This is where **Gibbs' reflective cycle** (1988) earns its keep. It's not a classroom exercise. It's a structured way to step back and figure out what's really going on when motivation or morale dips.

Here's how it breaks down:

1. **Description**: What's actually happening? (Missed deadlines? Silence in the mess deck?)
2. **Feelings**: What's the emotional landscape? (Frustration? Apathy? Short fuses?)
3. **Evaluation**: What's working and what isn't?
4. **Analysis**: What's really driving the slump? (Burnout? Lack of clarity? Weak leadership?)
5. **Conclusion**: What needs to change?
6. **Action plan**: What are you going to do differently from tomorrow?

It's structured common sense. Whether you're leading sailors, warehouse staff, software teams or apprentices, it helps you diagnose before you prescribe.

Think of it like a system check on morale. You don't just notice something's wrong and start swapping parts at random.

You slow down, observe, ask the right questions and then act. No assumptions, no fluff. Just tuned-in leadership.

15.4: Incentives that work

Morale doesn't live in policy documents. It lives in small, human experiences, often unplanned, but well timed. In the Navy, one of the best morale boosters was simple: going ashore. A few hours off the ship, a pub meal, a stretch of legs on dry land. That was enough to reset the whole team. No one expected it, but when it came, it mattered.

In the workplace, it's the same. It doesn't need to be fancy:

- Finish a tough sprint? Give the team a long weekend.
- Nail a project launch? Host a no-agenda team lunch.
- Meet targets early? Buy the next coffee round or chuck someone a voucher.

But let's be clear, not every bit of work needs a reward. We're all there to do a job. People work to get paid, to progress, to build skills or support their families. Showing up and grafting is part of the deal.

Incentives aren't about bribery or treating people like children. They're about timing, thoughtfulness and respect, or a quiet gesture that says, 'I saw what that cost you. And I appreciate it.'

Used well, they don't create entitlement; they create energy. And that's worth more than any bonus scheme.

15.5: Motivation vs manipulation

Let's talk about a line many leaders tiptoe across: manipulation. The truth is that all leadership is influence. And sometimes, a smart nudge at the right moment, done ethically, is exactly what your team needs. It's not sinister – it's an emotionally intelligent strategy.

For example: 'If we hit this milestone, I'll take care of lunch on Friday.'

That's not manipulation in the bad sense. It's soft influence, tapping into what someone values to help drive action. Motivation becomes manipulation only when it's sneaky, one-sided or dishonest.

Here's the difference:

- ⚓ Motivation is transparent. It's a nudge that respects choice.
- ⚓ Manipulation is controlling. It hides the real reason and removes choice.

Ethical influence means guiding your team by connecting effort with reward in a way that matters to them. It could be autonomy, recognition, learning opportunities, or just a cuppa and a thank you.

I once worked with a logistics supervisor who had a high turnover problem. His team was burned out and disengaged. He kept pushing targets harder, but they weren't listening any more.

After some tough feedback, he changed approach: weekly check-ins, spot rewards for accuracy, rotating tasks to break monotony. Within two months, productivity rose. But more importantly, trust returned.

What changed? Not the workload. The leadership.

People won't always remember the task. But they will remember how you made them feel while they were doing it.

Chapter 16

Leading change

We were on patrol in the Caribbean when one of the four main generators, a beast of an engine, needed a full, top-end overhaul. We were due alongside in 24 hours, so the plan was simple: strip it at sea, finish the rebuild in harbour, then enjoy a few cold beers and some sunshine. The lads had earned it. In six solid hours, we had the thing stripped, prepped and ready for parts. Job squared away. Beach calling. Sorted.

Then came the pipe: all bets off. We were being re-tasked. A hurricane was bearing down on a remote island to the north, and we had to get in position for possible aid and disaster relief. The mood shifted instantly. You could feel it. No cocktails, no downtime – just a fresh set of orders and rough seas ahead.

The problem? We had a generator mid-overhaul, tools everywhere, parts exposed. It was a hazard now, not a help. We had no choice but to spend another five hours rebuilding the thing, not to fix it, just to make it safe. All that progress, binned.

That's leadership in a crisis. You don't get to finish the plan. You do what the moment demands, even when it stings.

16.1: When change hits

One minute you're steaming toward a jetty and a beer; the next, you're frantically rebuilding a still-broken engine because a storm's coming. That's change. It doesn't wait for permission. It doesn't ask if now's convenient. It just kicks the door in and says, 'Right then, crack on.'

In the RN, change is constant: new orders, new missions, new bosses, new systems. You adapt or you get left behind.

It's no different in the civilian world:

- a restructure with no warning
- a new boss with a new way
- a system overhaul that kills productivity
- a customer base that vanishes overnight.

Change can feel like whiplash. Maybe your carefully planned week unravelled before lunch. It frustrates, confuses and, if mishandled, it torpedoes morale. But here's the truth: your credibility isn't built when things are easy. It's built when the deck shifts beneath your feet.

To lead change well, you don't need a perfect plan. You need presence. You need honesty. You need backbone. Start here:

- **Be clear:** Say what's changing, why, and what it means – no spin, no fluff.
- **Show empathy:** Change hits people differently. Make time to listen, even if you can't fix everything.
- **Stay adaptable:** Some parts of the plan will work; others won't. Adjust without losing the mission.
- **Hold the line:** Change adds chaos. Your job is to steady the ship. Set expectations and keep routines where you can.

Change doesn't care about your calendar. But your team cares how you handle it. Do it well and they'll follow you through the next storm, too.

16.2: Innovation or irrelevance

In leadership, change without innovation is just noise. You'll shift the deckchairs, but the ship still sinks. It becomes busy work – activity with no progress.

To lead meaningful change, you've got to:

- **create space for new ideas** – not just from the top, but from the deck plates
- **reward experimentation** – even when the first try flops
- **challenge the sacred cows** – the 'we've always done it this way' crew

- **protect dissenters** – because smart breakthroughs often start with awkward questions.

This isn't change for change's sake – it's purposeful evolution. So, this topic is a personal bugbear of mine. I spent time working within the Navy's own engineering school, alongside civilian contractors, many of them ex-Navy. You'd think they'd be keen to pass on their hard-earned experience. But instead, some refused to move with the times. They stuck to teaching what they were comfortable with: outdated systems, kit no longer in service, methods that no longer applied. Worse still, they constantly harked back to 'the good old days', banging on about how the Navy used to be, as if anything modern was inferior.

That's not helpful. That's dangerous. Instead of preparing trainees for real-world systems, they were anchoring them in the past. You can't steer a ship by staring at the wake.

Leadership means keeping one eye on what works now and the other on what's coming over the horizon. That tension between stability and change is where good leaders live.

16.3: Leading with less

There's never enough: not enough spares, not enough hands, not enough time. So, you adapt. You triage. You lead with what you've got, not what you wish you had.

You figure out:

- what matters
- how to prioritise under pressure
- how to innovate when the toolbox is empty.

Sound familiar? Civilian leaders hit the same wall: budget cuts, burned-out teams, supply chain gaps, hiring freezes. The difference between a stressed-out manager and a battle-ready leader? One complains, the other gets creative.

Here's how you lead through constraint:

- Focus on outcomes, not processes.
- Cut the fluff. Simplify wherever you can.
- Empower people to do more with less and trust them to get creative.

- Model calmness, because panic is contagious.

You can't always control what you have, but you can control how you lead.

16.4: Resistance isn't the problem – silence is

People don't hate change. They hate loss – of control, of stability, of identity. If you ignore that, you don't get buy-in – you get quiet rebellion. People nod, smile, then go back to doing things the old way, until your initiative dies a slow, silent death.

So, what do you do?

- **Name the discomfort**: 'I know this isn't easy.'
- **Communicate relentlessly:** 'Here's what's changing. Here's what's not.'
- **Invite input:** 'What do you need from me to make this work?'

Change works when people feel like they're part of it, not just victims of it.

Chapter 17

Leadership under personal pressure

Pressure doesn't wait for your schedule. It doesn't care how experienced you are, how well the plan was written or whether you've had any sleep. It just turns up and, suddenly, all eyes are on you. That's when leadership gets real. Not in team-building sessions or strategy workshops, but in the messy, silent moments when something's gone wrong and everyone's waiting to see how you react.

This chapter is about what happens when you're tired, short on answers and must still lead. When your mate's morale is shot, the chain of command is stressed and you're the one expected to keep it together.

Because that's the job.

17.1: Age isn't the issue

Leadership doesn't always show up in the package people expect. Sometimes the person in charge is 25. Other times, they're 55 and reporting to someone half their age. That alone can turn heads, stir up opinions and test egos.

I've seen young leaders step into rooms full of people older than them, often more experienced, sometimes more qualified on paper. And instantly, the barriers go up: resistance, sarcasm, silence. People are generally sceptical, but not always unfriendly. It's a natural human reaction: people question what they don't expect. Part of it is protective pride; no one wants to feel as if their years of experience are being disregarded. But the real issue is ego, not age.

You'll see the same thing in civilian life. A fresh-faced manager walks in, eager to get started, and suddenly people who've 'been here 20 years' start asking themselves, 'Why is this kid in charge of me?' The unspoken question is less about competence and more about legitimacy.

What matters isn't your age. It's your clarity, your humility and how well you align people around a shared purpose. That's what earns respect.

In both the Navy and civilian world, age doesn't always match authority. You'll see it all the time. People join the RN anywhere between 16 and their thirties – school leavers, career changers, uni grads. Everyone starts at the bottom, but progression depends on your trade, performance and opportunity. So, it's common to find a 23-year-old officer leading a department that includes 40-year-old SRs with double the sea time. That can get awkward fast, especially if egos aren't managed.

If you're that younger leader and want to be taken seriously, here's what to remember:

- **Acknowledge experience in the room:** Look around and ask, 'What knowledge is already here? Who's been through this before?' That doesn't mean deferring every decision; it means showing respect for those who've walked the road before you.
- **Lead through action, not volume:** Talking loudly or throwing your weight around doesn't make you a leader. It makes you look like a knob. Let your actions speak first.
- **Balance confidence with humility:** There's a fine line between being self-assured and being arrogant. Walk it with care.
- **Stay open to feedback:** You asked for the responsibility, so own the learning curve. If someone pulls you aside and says 'You could've handled that better', then listen. That's not a personal attack – it's a leadership gift.

But this isn't just a one-way street. You might be in your late thirties, finally promoted, and now leading a team of 18- to

21-year-olds – people quicker with systems, tech or modern processes. Suddenly *you* feel out of place. Your experience might be extensive, but it doesn't stop you feeling like the dinosaur in the room.

The same rules apply in reverse:

- **Don't patronise:** Respect goes both ways. They may not have your years, but they're bringing something else to the table.
- **Don't posture:** You don't need to puff up to prove yourself. Let your experience speak through calm, measured leadership.
- **Use your knowledge to develop others:** Help them avoid the mistakes you made. That's the role of a mentor, not a gatekeeper.
- **Stay open to new ideas:** You might not understand their approach immediately but give it a chance. The blend of youth and experience often produces the strongest outcomes.

At the end of the day, the best teams don't obsess over age. They focus on outcomes and how to get there together. Ego gets in the way of that. Respect, humility and intent get you back on course.

17.2: From mates to manager

Few things test your leadership like getting promoted over a peer, especially someone you'd consider a mate. Picture this: two JRs, great mates, same age, same intake, same bunk space. They've learned, worked and grown together. They've dodged the same rollockings and shared the same laughs in the mess. Then one of them is promoted to leading hand... and the other isn't. Things get awkward, fast.

Suddenly, there's a shift. Conversations feel different. Jokes aren't as easy. Maybe there's a bit of resentment. Maybe it's jealousy. Maybe it's just the simple fact that everything's changed, but no one quite knows how to talk about it.

It happens on civvy street, too. Two mates from the warehouse floor, and one gets the nod to be team leader. Now they're running the toolbox talks, signing off leave forms and pulling up people on standards, including their mate. One minute you're having a brew together; the next, you're being accused of 'forgetting where you came from'.

This dynamic is one of the hardest shifts in early leadership. You've already got enough going on in your first leadership role, figuring out authority, building confidence, learning new expectations. Having to second-guess how your mate feels on top of that? It's a recipe for stress, guilt and poor decisions.

You might not want to say it out loud, but here's the truth that needs accepting:

- ⚓ **Promotions reflect professional growth, not personal worth:** You didn't stab anyone in the back. You stepped up, simple as that.
- ⚓ **If the friendship's solid, it'll bend, not break:** Good mates understand that roles change. Great ones back you anyway.
- ⚓ **If it doesn't survive?** Then the cracks were already there. The promotion just made them visible.

If you're in this position, new to leadership and leading a mate, don't bury your head in the sand. Deal with it early, clearly and respectfully:

- ⚓ **Acknowledge the shift:** Don't pretend nothing's changed. Say something like, 'Look, I know this might feel weird for both of us, but I'm going to do my best to handle this role fairly and professionally.'
- ⚓ **Set boundaries (with empathy):** You can still care about your mate, but the job comes first now. Banter is fine until it undermines your authority. Draw that line early and explain why.
- ⚓ **Stay consistent:** The fastest way to lose respect is to play favourites or to go too far the other way and be overly harsh to prove you're not. Treat everyone fairly, including your mate.
- ⚓ **Don't carry guilt:** You didn't *do* something to them. You achieved something. Let that land.
- ⚓ **Earn respect from scratch:** Just because your mate respected you as an AB doesn't mean they'll respect you as a leader. That's normal. Lead well and let your actions rebuild that trust over time.

- ⚓ **Give them space:** They might need time to adjust. Let them. You're not in charge of how they feel, only how you lead.

You don't need to apologise for stepping up. And if you lead with fairness, consistency and clarity, you might just end up strengthening the friendship, not losing it.

But leadership means doing what's right for the team, even when it's uncomfortable. So, lead like a grown-up, not like a mate in uniform. That's how you earn respect and keep it.

17.3: Leadership in uncertainty

Uncertainty is leadership's proving ground. When the plan changes, the kit breaks, or your team takes a knock, how you respond defines your leadership.

In the RN, uncertainty is normal. One minute you're deploying to the Caribbean to provide humanitarian aid; 24 hours later, you're rerouted to a war zone with no return date. I've been there. You go from 'grab your sunglasses' to 'check your gas mask is in date' before the kettle's even boiled.

It's not just mission shifts. Kit can fail without warning. Lose propulsion? You're dead in the water. Radar drops out? You're sailing blind. Then throw in weather, rough seas, high humidity, arctic blasts, none of which care about your best-laid plans. And when half your team is fighting seasickness, morale dives with the temperature.

But uncertainty is not only external. It hits your people, too. Illness, family emergencies, mental fatigue, interpersonal conflict – all of it affects performance. It can be hard for sailors to focus as it would be for anyone if a close family member is rushed into hospital and they are on the other side of the globe.

That's the human side of uncertainty. And it's your job as a leader to steer the team through it.

So how do you lead in uncertainty?

- ⚓ **Stay grounded:** First and foremost, stay calm. Your team takes their emotional cue from you. If you lose your cool, they'll follow suit. But if you stay composed, even when the situation's shifting fast, they'll steady themselves on your tone. This doesn't mean pretending everything's fine. It means being the ballast in the storm. Reassure them that a plan is forming, even if you're building it as you go.

- ⚓ **Communicate early and often:** Silence breeds fear. Speak up. Be honest about what you know, what you don't and what you're doing to get answers. Your people don't expect you to be omniscient; they expect you to be honest and present.
- ⚓ **Acknowledge the disruption:** Address the emotional side too: 'I know this isn't what anyone expected.' Then shift the focus: 'Here's what we can control. Let's crack on with that.'
- ⚓ **Lead with empathy, not emotion:** Empathy is strength. Panic is weakness. Understand how uncertainty is affecting the team, but don't let emotions drive the ship. Recognise frustration, disappointment or fear, but keep the focus on what's next, not what's been lost.

If someone's struggling, pull them aside. Give them space. Then bring them back into the mission. No one wants to be sidelined; they want to be understood and guided.

Remind your team of what they've overcome before. Resilience does not mean never breaking; it's about remembering you've bounced back before, and you can do it again.

And when you need to show disappointment (because let's be honest, we all feel it sometimes), do it once. Briefly. Then move on. 'Gutted we're not going home. But we've got a job to do. Let's do it right.'

Uncertainty is the real test of leadership. Anyone can manage when things are ticking along. But when the lights go out, the mission changes or the team's rattled, that's when they look to you.

Lead like they'll remember this moment, because they will.

17.4: Mental health isn't optional

This one's personal... I've dealt with mental health issues since my teens. Depression isn't something I 'had'; it's still very much part of my day-to-day life. It doesn't clock off. It's an ongoing battle to keep things in check. And if you've ever been through it yourself, you know exactly what I mean. You don't always see it coming. You just wake up one day and realise you're struggling to do the basics – eat, sleep, think, feel like yourself.

I'm not a doctor. I'm not a therapist. And I'm definitely not writing this as some kind of expert. But I've lived it. I've led through it. I've seen it wreck careers, relationships, even lives, both in the Navy and in civvy street. I've also seen what happens when it's acknowledged, managed and supported.

Mental health isn't a weakness. It's a reality. And if you're going to lead, you need to take it seriously – yours and your team's. It starts with you.

Leadership doesn't mean pretending everything's fine. It means being honest with yourself first, by asking:

- How's my stress level?
- Am I sleeping?
- Do I snap at people?
- Am I drinking more than usual?
- Am I avoiding stuff I normally take in my stride?

These aren't just off days. They can be early warning signs. And the sooner you notice them, the better.

One of the hardest things to admit as a leader is that you're not OK. But leadership doesn't mean carrying everything alone. It means having the guts to say 'I need support' before things fall apart.

If you're worried about your own mental health, get help. Not when it's unbearable – now, before the wheels come off. You wouldn't ignore a fire in the engine room; you'd deal with it. Your headspace deserves the same attention. You can't lead if your head's not right.

You can't help others if you're falling apart yourself. It doesn't mean you're soft. It means you're smart enough and strong enough to get the help you need before it's too late.

17.5: Leading when others are struggling

Living and working in close quarters, on ships, on sites or on pressure-cooker projects, takes its toll. I've seen strong sailors break after long deployments. I've seen high-performing civvies collapse from burnout. The stress of constant output, family separation, sleep deprivation and zero downtime adds up fast.

People crack in different ways. Some lash out. Some go quiet.

Some drift and become unreliable, distracted, withdrawn. If someone on your team is suddenly off their game, don't ignore it. You might just save a career or even a life.

You are not a therapist. You are a leader. And that means your role is to notice, listen and signpost to the right support, not to fix.

You're responsible for creating an environment where people feel safe to speak up, and for taking it seriously when they do. You're also responsible for making sure that performance pressure never outweighs personal wellbeing.

The priority is always the person, not the job. If someone is struggling, the mission can wait. People come first. Full stop.

What you *can* do:

- **Create safe spaces:** Let people know they can talk. And mean it. If someone speaks in confidence, keep it unless there's a safety concern.
- **Know the signs:** Look for burnout, withdrawal, irritability, out-of-character mistakes.
- **Normalise rest:** Recovery isn't a luxury. It's essential.
- **Stop glorifying 'cracking on':** There's courage in pausing, too.
- **Signpost support:** Don't take it on yourself. Encourage them to speak to a medical professional, welfare rep or HR. That's leadership, not weakness.

If you believe someone may be at risk of harming themselves or others, you have a duty to act. Escalate it immediately, up the chain of command, to HR or to medical support. This isn't breaking trust. It's protecting life.

Mental health isn't a side issue; it's mission critical. High-performing teams don't just need strategy and skills. They need space to recover, support and humanity.

You're not there to treat. You're there to care and guide people towards proper help, before it's too late – no shame, no stigma. Put the person first, always. The rest can wait.

17.6: Complexity and conflicting priorities

As a leader, how you respond to challenges and frustrations sets the tone for everyone around you. Let's be honest, we've all had that moment where we snapped at a senior. Not out of malice, but pure frustration. Maybe they didn't have the full picture. Maybe they'd been behind a desk too long. Whatever the reason, the reaction wasn't our best. And if you're anything like me, you've probably replayed that moment for days.

Dwelling doesn't help. What matters is what you do next.

Learning to reflect, not ruminate and staying focused on practical solutions helps you lead with clarity. Especially when morale dips, the rumour mill kicks in and priorities start pulling you in ten different directions.

Big organisations bring big complications: multiple stakeholders, conflicting goals, bureaucratic fog, pet projects with no clear value.

You've seen it: half a dozen 'owners' pulling in different directions. One chasing deadlines. Another chasing budget. One with a political agenda. And not even one of them thinking about the pressure they're putting on the people doing the work.

Sometimes it's unintentional; it's just how the machine runs. But it's still a pain in the arse.

Projects often get bogged down in layers of sign-off and 'he said, she said' politics. And don't get me started on steakholders (yep, I said steak). Half of them are just there to carve out the biggest slice for themselves, not to support the team or the outcome.

I've seen it in the RN. I've seen it in civvy street – decisions made by people miles away from the frontline, with no clue what's going on, but still holding sway. That's where chaos starts, especially in high-pressure environments where speed and unity matter.

So, what do good leaders do? They don't play the game; they change it:

- ⚓ They cut through the noise.
- ⚓ They bring clarity when others bring confusion.
- ⚓ They shield their teams from unnecessary chaos.
- ⚓ They align effort with purpose.

Not just activity for activity's sake, but action that delivers.

Complexity and conflicting priorities are part of the job. But they don't have to derail your team. Your job is to navigate the fog, keep your people focused and make sure it's not the frontline paying the price for disorganised leadership up top.

17.7: Productivity vs people

The anticipation of time off, whether after a long deployment or before summer holidays, can shift everything. Morale often peaks when people know a break is coming. Christmas, birthdays, family events – they remind your team there's more to life than work.

But let's face it: that excitement can also tank productivity. Focus drifts. People mentally check out. The job doesn't always get their full attention. And that's normal. So, now you have to balance output with empathy

You can't squeeze every drop of energy out of your team without giving them a chance to recharge. If you do, they'll break, and you'll be left wondering why no one's stepping up any more.

Here's how to stay ahead of the curve:

- ⚓ **Plan for downtime**: Don't pretend people won't slow down around leave periods. Build it into your schedule.
- ⚓ **Recognise effort:** A simple 'good job' goes a long way when people are running on fumes.
- ⚓ **Set expectations, then back off:** Be clear about what needs doing, but don't hover. Trust your team to manage the pace.

High-performing teams don't just push hard; they recover well. And they recover well because the environment allows them to. As a leader, it's your responsibility to balance the mission with the people doing the work. Your job is to drive outcomes without burning everyone out in the process. Because leadership is about more than what gets done. It's also about how your team feels while doing it. That's what builds real, sustainable performance.

Chapter 18

Leading in tough conditions

When the environment, structure or situation stacks the odds against you, leadership gets real. Some challenges hit without warning: a system crash, a serious injury, a mission change with zero notice.

Others are baked into the job: tight timelines, not enough people or kit, brutal conditions or a rigid command structure that leaves little room to manoeuvre. You don't get to choose the terrain, but you *do* get to choose how you lead on it.

This chapter gets into the thick of it: environmental stress, cultural friction, organisational gridlock and the emotional weight that comes with command – the messy, pressure-loaded reality that separates armchair theory from the kind of leadership that counts.

18.1: Operational disruption and uncertainty

Whether you're rerouted mid-deployment or your civvy team loses its biggest client overnight, unplanned change hits hard. It rattles focus. It kills momentum. It punches morale straight in the gut.

Some disruptions come out of nowhere: a system crash, a crew injury, a mission change at 03:00. You can't always see it coming. One minute you're two weeks into a calm Caribbean patrol, the next you're being rerouted to a live conflict zone for nine months. One system glitch and the radar's gone. One dodgy gearbox and propulsion's dead. The sick bay's full because the lads have diarrhoea and vomiting (D&V), the mess is short tempered and everyone's knackered from relentless shifts and weather that won't let up.

And it's no easier in civvy street. A key staff member walks mid-project. The market shifts. Your biggest client pulls out. Leadership reshuffles, budgets vanish or a last-minute change lands on your desk with the word 'urgent' attached.

The context changes, but the pressure doesn't.

Disruption is disruption. It doesn't care about your planning. It tests your leadership, not your admin.

So, what do you do?

⚓ **Stay calm:** Your tone becomes their tone. Panic spreads fast, but so does steady energy. Even if you don't have all the answers, don't lose your head. Your job is to show there's a way through.

⚓ **Communicate early:** Tell the team what you know and what you don't. Hiding the situation just feeds the rumour mill. Be honest about what's changing, and what's staying the same.

⚓ **Acknowledge emotion:** Disappointment? Frustration? Fair enough. Say it. Then crack on. Help the team process what's happened, but don't let them wallow. Re-focus them on what comes next.

⚓ **Draw on strengths:** Remind them of what they've handled before. Get people involved in finding solutions. That sense of progress, even if it's small, lifts morale *fast*.

⚓ **Don't make it about you:** You might be gutted too. Fair enough. But don't drag the team into your spiral. Vent in private. Lead in public.

You won't always control the disruption. But you *can* control your clarity. And that's what your team needs most: a leader who keeps their head when everything else is going sideways.

18.2: Mental strain in isolated environments

Living and working in close quarters for long periods grinds people down. The pressure, the distance from home, the relentless demand, it all stacks up.

It's easy to see this as a Navy-specific issue. And sure, being a sailor is far from normal. You live where you work. You're shoulder to shoulder with the same people every hour of the day, weeks at a time, in a metal box that never stops moving. It's a tough environment to lead in.

But step outside the Navy, and the pattern's still there, just with a different uniform. Take a small civvy shift team – nine hours a day, five days a week with the same faces, same quirks and same irritations building up over time. It might not feel extreme at first, but it adds up just the same. And when it does, it shows. Some withdraw. Some lash out. Some shut down emotionally, even if they're still turning up on time.

The signs are subtle at first: a sharp tone, a missed deadline, banter that suddenly lands flat. Left unchecked, it snowballs into resentment, burnout, conflict or even crisis.

What do you do? You lead like a human being. That means normalising the conversation, treating mental strain the same way you'd treat fatigue or injury (see the previous chapter for more on this). It means making space for people to talk, not in some formal sit-down, but in the rhythm of daily life, during briefs, stand-downs or just in passing. You step in early, before things escalate. A quiet word now is worth more than a formal intervention later. And most of all, you protect your people, not just from more work, but from the weight of unrealistic expectations. That's leadership.

18.3: When rumours take over

A whisper can sink a project faster than a missed deadline. The moment a plan looks shaky, the rumours start. Someone hears a scrap of information. Someone else fills in the blanks. Before long, the whole team's off task, off balance and making decisions based on guesswork instead of facts. Morale dips. Focus scatters. Trust erodes.

You'll see it in real time:

- The project's under review, and suddenly half the team stops investing.
- Leadership reshuffles are hinted at, and people start covering their backs.
- No one knows what's happening, but everyone has a theory.

It happens in uniform, too: one uncertain order, one unconfirmed tasking, one bit of silence from above. Before you know it, the mess deck's buzzing and half the ship's convinced you're heading into a worst-case scenario that may never come.

So, what do you do? You don't hide behind silence. That's the mistake most leaders make. They wait for answers, thinking it's safer not to say anything until it's official. But that silence? It gets filled with noise.

Here's what works instead:

- **Acknowledge the unknowns:** Be honest. Say 'This part's still up in the air' instead of pretending everything's fine.
- **Be transparent about what** is **known:** Anchoring the team with facts, even limited ones, helps to steady the ship.
- **Refocus attention on what's still solid:** What can the team control today? What's still needed right now? Lead them back to that.
- **Stay visible:** The less your team sees you, the more they'll assume the worst. You don't need all the answers – just show up.

Uncertainty is survivable; mixed signals are not.

When rumours take over, it's not the ambiguity that hurts your team; it's the silence. If you want to build trust in tough times, don't wait for clarity.

18.4: Bullying and harassment

Abusive behaviour doesn't start with fists. It starts with silence, snide comments, exclusion, intimidation and the team watching a leader do nothing about it.

Whether you're in a mess deck, a control room, an office or a workshop, bullying and harassment destroy morale, trust and performance. The damage is quiet at first: withdrawn team members, rising tension, broken trust. But left unchecked, it spreads fast and poisons everything you're trying to build.

Abuse isn't always loud or obvious. It shows up in offhand comments, digs passed off as banter or being left out of conversations without explanation. It's the kind of behaviour people pretend is harmless, but it's not. It's persistent, targeted and corrosive. And when it's ignored, it only gets worse.

It can look like:

- constantly undermining someone in front of others
- mocking or isolating someone because of who they are or how they think
- excluding someone from social or work-based conversations
- power games hidden behind 'just a joke'
- inappropriate remarks, touch or gestures brushed off with 'Come on, it's just a laugh'.

And harassment? It's not just sexual. It can be racial, cultural, gender-based or deeply personal. At its core, it's about making someone feel unsafe, unwelcome or as if they don't belong. If you see it and do nothing, you've allowed it. And in the eyes of your team? That makes you complicit.

It doesn't matter how sharp your technical skills are. If you can't create a safe environment, you're not leading. The longer this crap is left to fester, the more trust you lose, and the more damage is done.

What to watch out for? Well, sometimes it's obvious, sometimes it's subtle. Either way, you need to be paying attention to the following:

- a team member who goes quiet, avoids certain people or starts underperforming
- requests to change shifts, avoid certain roles or sit elsewhere
- banter that's always one sided or cruel
- a toxic team member everyone else tiptoes around.

If something feels off, it probably is. You don't need to launch a full investigation on the spot. But you do need to act:

- **Interrupt the behaviour immediately:** Stop it there and then. Don't laugh along. Don't ignore it.

- ⚓ **Speak to the person affected, privately:** Ask if they're OK. Let them know you saw it. Don't interrogate. Just listen.
- ⚓ **Log what you've seen:** Even if it doesn't go further yet, keep a record.
- ⚓ **Escalate when needed:** You're not expected to fix it alone. But you are expected to get support from HR, welfare, senior leadership.
- ⚓ **Don't make promises you can't keep:** Say this: 'I don't know the full picture, but I want to make sure you feel safe.' That alone builds trust.

You must take a zero-tolerance approach to bullying and harassment – no grey areas, no excuses. No one on your team gets to abuse, humiliate, intimidate or isolate someone else and still stay under your leadership.

End of story.

Chapter 19

Lifelong leadership

You don't stop leading when the uniform comes off or the title changes. Leadership is something you carry.

I've stood in engine rooms with alarms blaring and teams looking to me for calm. I've also stood in boardrooms with no rank to lean on, just reputation, responsibility and mindset. And that's the point. Leadership isn't military. It's not corporate. It's human.

It starts the moment you take responsibility. In the Navy, that meant owning your mistakes, backing your team under pressure and making decisions when there were no perfect options. In civilian life, it means holding the line when standards start to slip, choosing integrity when it's inconvenient and leading yourself first, before leading anyone else.

The core always transfers. Some things never expire: owning your actions, learning fast, listening between the lines, lifting your team and bouncing back stronger. Whether you're in a school, a start-up or a kitchen, these are the tools that work.

People don't follow charisma. They follow consistency. They follow when you do what you say, help them find purpose, mentor without ego and when you keep learning. You're not just solving problems; you're shaping future leaders. And that means staying sharp. Leadership stagnates when you stop learning. As I've said, the best leaders I've worked with and learned from were the ones who never acted as if they'd cracked it. They stayed curious, took feedback and adapted constantly.

Leadership isn't something you earn once. You earn it daily, through your choices, not your title.

Here's what that mindset looks like in practice – values I carried from the RN and still live by today:

- **Lead by example**: Your actions speak louder than your rank. Set the tone.
- **Stay calm in the storm**: Pressure reveals true leadership. Stay grounded.
- **Know your crew**: Understand their strengths, pressures and personalities.
- **Communicate clearly**: Clarity saves time, stress and lives.
- **Adapt and overcome**: Plans fail; leaders don't. Be flexible.
- **Get respect, don't demand it**: Earn it through consistency, not control.
- **Make decisions, don't dither:** Delay can be deadlier than a wrong call.
- **Train hard, fight easy:** The harder you train, the smoother the crisis.
- **Take responsibility:** Step up. Own the outcome. Lead from the front.
- **Keep morale high**: A supported crew is a high-performing crew.
- **Never stop learning**: If you're not learning, you're slipping.
- **Serve before self:** True leadership is about others, not ego.
- **Shipshape and Bristol fashion**: Details matter. Order reflects mindset.
- **Know when to listen**: you don't have all the answers – but your team might.

Leadership means showing up when it counts, asking the right questions and trusting the people around you. Whether you're on a warship, in a school, a workshop or a boardroom, the fundamentals stay the same: clarity, trust, adaptability and the courage to act.

This book hasn't offered a one-size-fits-all blueprint. Instead, it's shared a mindset, shaped by experience, pressure, mistakes and growth. You now have a toolkit to help you plan, prioritise, communicate and lead through change. Use it. Adapt it. Add to it.

Don't wait for someone to tell you you're ready. Leadership starts the moment you take responsibility for more than just yourself.

So go on, step up. Back your team. Make the call. Own the outcome. And lead the way.

You've got this.

Leadership isn't a finish line; it's a mindset. Keep growing. Keep showing up. And leave every team better than you found it.

As you close this book, remember:

1. Don't just use what you've read – live it.
2. Don't wait for permission; you're already leading.
3. Don't aim to be perfect; aim to be present.

Whether you're in combat boots or brogues, a tailored suit or scrubs, your mission stays the same:

Lead with integrity. Build people. Leave something better.

Further reading

The following sources informed the thinking and examples used throughout this book and are included for readers who want to explore these ideas in more depth.

Adair, J (1973) *Action-Centred Leadership*. McGraw-Hill Inc.

Bargh, J A, & Chartrand, T L (1999) 'The unbearable automaticity of being'. New York University. URL: acmelab.yale.edu/sites/default/files/1999_the_unbearable_automaticity_of_being.pdf

Bazerman, M H & Moore, D A (2013) *Judgment in Managerial Decision Making*. Wiley.

Bell, S (2025) 'The Eisenhower Matrix: Urgent vs important'. MindTools 25 July. URL: mindtools.com/al1e0k5/eisenhowers-urgentimportant-principle

Center for Creative Leadership (2019) *Feedback That Works: How to build and deliver your message*. CCL.

Chartered Institute of Personnel and Development (CIPD):

- 'Diversity, inclusion and organisational performance'. URL: cipd.org/uk/knowledge/factsheets/diversity-factsheet
- 'Employee communication'. URL: cipd.org/uk/knowledge/factsheets/employee-communication
- 'The role of emotions at work: Recognising the influence of emotions'. URL: cipd.org/uk/knowledge/bitesize-research/role-emotions
- Guidance on management tools and frameworks (including RACI, SMART objectives and SWOT analysis) – see cipd.org/uk/knowledge/tools
- Unconscious bias at work, podcast series. URL: cipd.org/uk/knowledge/podcasts/unconscious-bias

Driscoll, J (2007) *Practising Clinical Supervision: A reflective approach*. Bailliere Tindall.

Gibbs, G (1988) *Learning by Doing: A guide to teaching and learning methods*. Further Education Unit.

Goleman, D (1998) *What Makes a Leader?* Harvard Business Review Press.

Greenwald, A G & Banaji, M R (1995) 'Implicit social cognition: Attitudes, self-esteem and stereotypes'. URL: pubmed.ncbi.nlm.nih.gov/7878162

Harvard Business Review. 'A primer on OKRs'. URL: store.hbr.org/product/a-primer-on-okrs/123081

Kahneman, D (2011) *Thinking, Fast and Slow*. Penguin.

Lewin, K (1947) 'Frontiers in group dynamics: Concept, method and reality in social science; social equilibria and social change'. URL: journals.sagepub.com/doi/10.1177/001872674700100103

Maslach, C & Leiter, M P (2016) 'Understanding the burnout experience: Recent research and its implications for psychiatry'. World Psychiatry. URL: pmc.ncbi.nlm.nih.gov/articles/PMC4911781

McEwen, B S (2007) 'Physiology and neurobiology of stress and adaptation: Central role of the brain'. *Physiological Reviews*. URL: pubmed.ncbi.nlm.nih.gov/17615391

McKinsey & Company (2020) 'Diversity wins: How inclusion matters'. 19 May. URL:mckinsey.com/featured-insights/diversity-and-inclusion/diversity-wins-how-inclusion-matters

Mehrabian, A (1972) *Silent Messages: Implicit communication of emotions and attitudes*. Wadsworth Publishing Company.

National Museum of the Royal Navy. URL: nmrn.org.uk

NHS England Plan–Do–Study–Act (PDSA) Cycle. URL: england.nhs.uk/improvement-hub/wp-content/uploads/sites/44/2015/08/learning-handbook-pdsa.pdf

Page, S E (2007) *The Difference: How the power of diversity creates better groups, firms, schools, and societies*. Princeton University Press.

Tversky, A & Kahneman, D (1982) *Judgment under Uncertainty: Heuristics and biases*. Cambridge University Press.

UK Ministry of Defence (2023) 'Defence writing guide'. Development, Concepts and Doctrine Centre (DCDC). URL: assets.publishing.service.gov.uk/media/651d64d9bef21800156ded74/DCDC_Writers_Handbook.pdf

UK Ministry of Defence (2022) 'UK defence doctrine' (6th ed). URL: assets.publishing.service.gov.uk/media/63776f4de90e0728553b568b/UK_Defence_Doctrine_Ed6.pdf

Appendix A

What sort of leader are you?

How it works: For each statement, circle the number that best reflects how you usually lead. 1 = Strongly disagree | 2 = Disagree | 3 = Neutral | 4 = Agree | 5 = Strongly agree

Autocratic leader

I prefer making decisions without consulting others.

□ 1 □ 2 □ 3 □ 4 □ 5

I expect my team to follow instructions without question.

□ 1 □ 2 □ 3 □ 4 □ 5

I use a clear, top-down approach when leading.

□ 1 □ 2 □ 3 □ 4 □ 5

I avoid group discussions that slow things down.

□ 1 □ 2 □ 3 □ 4 □ 5

Total score for autocratic leader: ______ /20

Bureaucratic leader

I stick closely to established procedures and rules.

□ 1 □ 2 □ 3 □ 4 □ 5

I prefer formal processes to manage conflict.

□ 1 □ 2 □ 3 □ 4 □ 5

I value a clear chain of command.

□ 1 □ 2 □ 3 □ 4 □ 5

I get uncomfortable when things deviate from protocol.

□ 1 □ 2 □ 3 □ 4 □ 5

Total score for bureaucratic leader: _____ /20

Charismatic leader

I motivate others by passionately sharing a vision.

□ 1 □ 2 □ 3 □ 4 □ 5

People look to me for inspiration and direction.

□ 1 □ 2 □ 3 □ 4 □ 5

I use stories or personal experience to connect with others.

□ 1 □ 2 □ 3 □ 4 □ 5

I'm energised by being in front of a group.

□ 1 □ 2 □ 3 □ 4 □ 5

Total score for charismatic leader: ______ /20

Democratic leader

I encourage everyone to share ideas before decisions are made.
□ 1 □ 2 □ 3 □ 4 □ 5

I believe all team members deserve a voice.
□ 1 □ 2 □ 3 □ 4 □ 5

When possible, I aim for group consensus.
□ 1 □ 2 □ 3 □ 4 □ 5

I regularly ask for feedback on my leadership.
□ 1 □ 2 □ 3 □ 4 □ 5

Total score for democratic leader:
______ /20

Laissez-faire leader

I trust people to find their own solutions.
□ 1 □ 2 □ 3 □ 4 □ 5

I prefer not to micromanage or supervise.
□ 1 □ 2 □ 3 □ 4 □ 5

I believe autonomy leads to better results.
□ 1 □ 2 □ 3 □ 4 □ 5

I let people take full ownership of their work.
□ 1 □ 2 □ 3 □ 4 □ 5

Total score for laissez-faire leader:
______ /20

Servant leader

I help my team grow personally and professionally.
□ 1 □ 2 □ 3 □ 4 □ 5

I care more about people than just ticking off tasks.
□ 1 □ 2 □ 3 □ 4 □ 5

I listen to team concerns and act on them.
□ 1 □ 2 □ 3 □ 4 □ 5

I lead by example and put others first.
□ 1 □ 2 □ 3 □ 4 □ 5

Total score for servant leader:
______ /20

Transactional leader

I set clear expectations and goals.
□ 1 □ 2 □ 3 □ 4 □ 5

I reward performance and results.
□ 1 □ 2 □ 3 □ 4 □ 5

I hold people accountable for standards and deadlines.
□ 1 □ 2 □ 3 □ 4 □ 5

I believe incentives drive success.
□ 1 □ 2 □ 3 □ 4 □ 5

Total score for transactional leader:
______ /20

Transformational leader

I regularly share a bold vision for the future.
□ 1 □ 2 □ 3 □ 4 □ 5

I push others to think creatively and break new ground.
□ 1 □ 2 □ 3 □ 4 □ 5

I create growth opportunities for the team.
□ 1 □ 2 □ 3 □ 4 □ 5

I challenge norms and encourage innovation.
□ 1 □ 2 □ 3 □ 4 □ 5

Total score for transformational leader:
______ /20

Score interpretation guide

Use this table to interpret your score for each leadership style:

- 17–20: Strong preference – this may be your dominant leadership style.
- 13–16: Moderate use – you may rely on this style situationally.
- 9–12: Potential growth area – consider further development.
- 4–8: Least used – may reflect discomfort or lack of experience.

How to use your results

1. High score in a style: your dominant approach.
2. Lowest score: consider developing these areas.
3. Suggestions: seek feedback or mentorship based on your results.

Quick reference

- **Autocratic:** top down, directive.
- **Bureaucratic**: rule-following, structured.
- **Charismatic**: visionary, inspirational.
- **Democratic**: collaborative, consensus driven.
- **Laissez-faire**: hands off, independent.
- **Servant**: supportive, people first.
- **Transactional**: performance based, incentive focused.
- **Transformational**: visionary, growth oriented.

Appendix B

SWOT analysis

Example:

SWOT analysis: *Preparation for a coastal clean-up operation*	
Strengths (What my team does well)	**Weaknesses (What we can improve)**
Experienced in environmental clean-up projects. *Equipment (such as gloves, bags and tools) is ready and in good condition.* *Strong volunteers and community support.*	*Limited transportation for moving waste to the disposal site.* *Limited experience dealing with hazardous materials.* *New team members may require guidance.*
Opportunities (What could help us succeed)	**Threats (What could go wrong)**
Support from local businesses offering sponsorship or resources. *Media coverage to raise awareness of the clean-up effort.* *Partnerships with environmental organisations for additional expertise.*	*Bad weather on the clean-up day could delay the operation.* *Not enough volunteers showing up to complete the task.* *Potential safety hazards such as sharp objects or contaminated waste.*

SWOT tips:

- **Combine with SMART objectives:** Use SWOT outputs to shape SMART objectives (see Appendix C).
- **Collaborate with your team**: Complete SWOT with your team to avoid blind spots.

Appendix C

SMART objectives

SMART = specific, measurable, achievable, relevant and **time-bound.**

Example:

Objective: *Transfer medical supplies at sea*
Specific (state the goal in detail)
Safely transfer urgent medical supplies from our ship to a commercial fishing vessel using the ship's sea boat during a night deployment, completing the task within a one-hour window. A small, trained team conducts the transfer, with clear roles, tight communications, and the ship holding station to keep the operation controlled and safe.
Measurable (explain the outcome)
Medical supplies are transferred without damage or loss. The operation is completed within the planned time window. The team and equipment return safely to the ship, with launch, transfer and recovery conducted in a controlled and well-communicated sequence.
Achievable (ensure you have all you need)
The sea boat is prepared and seaworthy, supplies are secured and a trained team is available. Conditions are suitable for a night operation, with contingency procedures in place.
Relevant (does it align with broader goals?)
Supports maritime safety and builds trust through providing assistance when required.
Time-bound (set a deadline)
Complete the task within a defined one-hour operational window, including preparation, transfer and recovery.

Appendix D

Eisenhower Matrix

As a leader, you're constantly juggling tasks and responsibilities. The Eisenhower Matrix is a tool that helps you sort tasks based on urgency and importance. It categorises tasks into four quadrants.

Objective: Organising first aid training

<table>
<tr><th></th><th>Urgent</th><th>Not urgent</th></tr>
<tr><td>Important</td><td>Do First
Confirm the venue booking by Friday to secure the space.
Finalise the list of certified instructors and ensure they're available.</td><td>Schedule
Develop the training schedule, including breaks and activity sessions.
Create promotional materials and schedule social media posts two weeks before the event.</td></tr>
<tr><td>Not Important</td><td>Delegate
Assign a team member to send reminder emails to participants a week before the event.
Delegate ordering training supplies (such as first aid kits) to the logistics officer.</td><td>Eliminate
Spending time designing overly detailed event decorations.
Checking the event website multiple times a day when it's already finalised.</td></tr>
</table>

Appendix E

Communication styles cheat sheet

It's not just what you say, it's how you say it. This cheat sheet gives quick, practical guidance on communicating with clarity, respect and authority.

Core communication styles		
Style	**Traits**	**When to use**
Assertive	Clear, confident, respectful	Default mode: giving direction, setting standards
Passive	Hesitant, avoids conflict	Rarely, can confuse or reduce your authority
Aggressive	Forceful, hostile, reactive	Only in emergencies when immediate action is needed
Passive–aggressive	Sarcastic, indirect, resentful	Never – corrodes trust and morale

Tone and phrase tips		
Situation	**Say this**	**Not this**
Setting direction	'Here's what success looks like today.'	'Just do what I told you.'
Giving feedback	'Here's what I noticed – let's improve it.'	'You've messed this up again.'
Building trust	'I appreciate your input; it helps us grow.'	'That's not how we do things here.'
Clarifying confusion	'Let's walk through this together.'	'Didn't you read the brief?'

Body language reminders	
Cue	**What it signals**
Eye contact	Confidence and connection
Open posture	Approachability and calm authority
Crossed arms	Defensiveness or disinterest
Fidgeting/pacing	Stress, distraction or discomfort

Quick fixes for common mistakes		
If you're feeling...	**Don't do this**	**Try this instead**
Frustrated	Sarcasm or stone-walling	Pause, breathe, ask for a moment
Under pressure	Bark orders without context	State the priority and why it matters
Disrespected	Snap or escalate	Reset the tone, address it directly later
Ignored	Repeat louder or with blame	Ask: 'Is now a good time to go over this?'

Appendix F

Situational leadership quick reference

There's no one-size-fits-all approach to leadership. This cheat sheet helps you match your leadership style to the task, the team and the moment.

Situational leadership matrix		
Situation	**Best-fit style(s)**	**What that looks like**
Crisis/ emergency	Autocratic	Take control, issue clear instructions, act decisively. There's no time for debate
Burnout or low morale	Servant, transformational	Show care, listen deeply, reframe the mission to reconnect with purpose
Planning a new project	Democratic, transformational	Facilitate ideas, build buy-in, set an inspiring direction together
Training new recruits	Bureaucratic, transactional	Lay down structure, teach procedures, give regular corrective feedback and rewards
Skilled, high-performing team	Laissez-faire, servant	Step back, give them ownership, remove obstacles and let them run
Cross-functional collaboration	Democratic, charismatic	Build shared goals, manage competing interests, energise the group with clear vision

Flexing your leadership style:

- **Ask:** Who's in front of me? What do they need – clarity, freedom, support, direction?
- **Check:** Am I leading this way because it fits or because it's what I always do?
- **Shift:** Adjust in real time based on feedback, energy and what's getting results.

Common traps to avoid	
Trap	**Better approach**
Leading everyone the same	Tune your style to each person's confidence and competence
Overcorrecting after failure	Support with guardrails, not handcuffs; coach, don't control
Waiting too long to adapt	Check in early, don't wait for failure to realise the style mismatch

Think of leadership styles like engine settings: you don't swap engines, you adjust the throttle. The right setting at the right time keeps your team moving smoothly.

Appendix G

Delegation tips

Clear, practical steps to help you delegate with confidence and clarity.

Step	Focus	What to Check
1	**Pick the task**	Does it free you up to lead? Can someone else learn from it?
2	**Pick the person**	Do they have the skill, capacity, or stretch potential?
3	**Set the standard**	What does 'done' look like? By when? Any limits?
4	**Share the context**	Why it matters. Who's affected. What to watch for.
5	**Hand over ownership**	They own delivery. You don't hover.
6	**Trust and step back**	No micromanaging. Silence shows trust.
7	**Check in, don't take over**	Light-touch updates. Praise what works. Correct early.

Quick reminder

- ⚓ Delegate to develop, not just to survive.
- ⚓ Avoid overloading your 'go-to' person.
- ⚓ Fair workload builds trust; favouritism kills it.
- ⚓ Ask yourself: Who else could grow from this?

Appendix H

Reflection tools

Leadership demands a lot, mentally and emotionally. These short prompts help you reset, refocus and lead with clarity, in the moment, after an event or during a short debrief.

They're especially useful after:

- team tension or breakdowns
- high-stakes decisions
- times when you felt 'off' as a leader
- morale dips or misreads
- signs of personal fatigue or burnout.

Use them alone, in supervision or to centre yourself before a critical interaction.

Check	Ask yourself
Tone check	Is the team reacting to the situation... or to me?
Pause check	Am I responding, or just reacting?
People check	Who needs reassurance, clarity or backing right now?
Energy check	Am I running on fumes? What's my reset plan?
Learning check	What worked today? What will I do differently next time?

If you want to go one layer deeper ask yourself:

- Am I bringing calm or chaos into the room?
- Would I want to follow me in this state?
- Is anyone going quiet who's usually solid?
- What's the one lesson I'm carrying forward?

Glossary of leadership and naval terms

Military and naval terms

- **AB (able rate):** A junior enlisted sailor in the RN. Roughly equivalent to a team member or frontline worker.
- **Alongside:** When a ship is alongside, it is berthed next to a jetty or dock rather than at sea. Often used more broadly to describe harbour periods, maintenance phases or time alongside between deployments.
- **Bridge:** The ship's command and navigation centre. Comparable to an operational HQ or control room.
- **CO (commanding officer):** The officer in command of the ship or unit. Ultimately responsible for performance, discipline, safety and mission delivery, similar to a chief executive or overall head of an organisation.
- **CPO (chief petty officer):** A senior non-commissioned officer (NCO) in charge of technical and leadership responsibilities. Similar to a senior manager or department head.
- **Chain of command:** The formal hierarchy that outlines authority and responsibility in any organisation.
- **Clear lower deck:** A mandatory all-hands briefing or announcement. No one's dodging this one.
- **Damage control:** Shipboard emergency procedures for fire, flood or structural issues. Used metaphorically in leadership for handling crises.
- **Divisional system:** The Navy's personnel and welfare structure. Combines HR, welfare, admin and discipline under divisional leadership.

- **DMEO:** Deputy marine engineering officer.
- **Jack speak:** Naval slang and mess-deck banter, unique to RN culture.
- **Killick**: Informal slang for a leading hand. A junior team leader or supervisor.
- **Kit-mustered:** a rigorous inspection where sailors, particularly recruits in training, must lay out their entire issued uniform and equipment in a precise, standardised pattern.
- **LH (leading hand):** A junior leader, like a shift supervisor or team lead.
- **Mess deck:** Communal area for eating, socialising and informal leadership moments.
- **MEM:** Marine engineering mechanic.
- **MEO (marine engineering officer):** The senior engineer on board, responsible for propulsion, maintenance and ship systems.
- **MCMV (mine countermeasures vessel):** A specialist Navy ship focused on mine detection and clearance.
- **Pipe:** A tannoy announcement or broadcast made over the ship's main communication system.
- **PO (petty officer):** A mid-ranking NCO responsible for team execution and technical oversight.
- **OOW (officer of the watch):** The officer in charge of ship operations and navigation during a specific duty watch.
- **RAS (replenishment at sea):** A complex operation to transfer fuel, equipment or people between ships while moving. A metaphor for coordination, interdependence and trust in fast-paced environments.
- **RFA (Royal Fleet Auxiliary):** Civilian-staffed support ships that provide logistics and supplies to the RN.
- **RIB (rigid inflatable boat):** A fast boat used for boarding, rescue or shore access.
- **SR (senior rate):** Any senior NCO (such as a PO or CPO) tasked with leading, mentoring and running departments.
- **Run ashore:** Slang for heading out for a break, often on land after a long period at sea.
- **Shit deflector:** Mess-deck slang for a senior who shields their team from pressure, politics or plain old blame. A respected leadership trait.

- **Sitrep (situation report):** A short update on status or conditions. Also used in civilian project reporting.
- **Upper deck:** The top deck of a ship. Can also refer to physical or metaphorical visibility and exposure.
- **Voluntold:** Being 'volunteered' for something without a real say. Classic Navy sarcasm.
- **Watch:** A duty rotation or shift that keeps operations running 24/7.
- **Wardroom:** The mess and social space for officers on board ship. Also used to refer to the officer community more broadly.
- **WR:** Warfare rating.
- **XO (executive officer):** The ship's second in command. Handles discipline, daily routines and operational management.

Leadership and organisational terms

- **Unconscious bias:** Automatic mental shortcuts that influence judgement and behaviour without conscious awareness.
- **Cognitive bias:** Systematic patterns of flawed thinking that affect decision making.
- **Psychological safety:** A shared belief that it's safe to speak up, ask questions or admit mistakes without fear of punishment.
- **Burnout:** A state of emotional, mental and physical exhaustion caused by prolonged stress and overload.
- **Emotional labour:** The effort involved in managing emotions – your own and others' – as part of a leadership role.
- **Resilience:** The ability to absorb pressure, adapt and recover while remaining effective.
- **Mission command:** A leadership philosophy based on clear intent, decentralised decision making and trust.
- **Situational leadership:** Adapting leadership style based on an individual's competence and confidence.
- **Span of control:** The number of people a leader is directly responsible for.
- **Delegation vs abdication:** The difference between assigning responsibility with oversight and abandoning accountability.

About the author

Christopher Dodd is a former chief petty officer in the Royal Navy with nearly 19 years of service. During his career, he led teams in high-pressure, high-responsibility environments, from engine room emergencies to operational deployments, where decisions carried real consequences for people, equipment and mission success.

His approach to leadership was shaped on the lower deck and built through real experience rather than theory alone. Over the years, he learned that trust, clarity and accountability matter far more than rank, noise or ego. He led at every level, made mistakes, learned from poor leadership as well as good and carried those lessons into civilian life.

He wrote *Navigating Leadership* for people stepping into leadership roles without a manual, confidence or all the answers. His aim is simple: to give new and aspiring leaders a practical, honest guide to leading well when it counts.